DEVELOPMENT CENTRE STUDIES

THE INFORMAL SECTOR
...ID 1990s

...E
...RATION AND DEVELOPMENT

Pursuant to Article 1 of the Convention signed in Paris on 14th December 1960, and which came into force on 30th September 1961, the Organisation for Economic Co-operation and Development (OECD) shall promote policies designed:

— to achieve the highest sustainable economic growth and employment and a rising standard of living in Member countries, while maintaining financial stability, and thus to contribute to the development of the world economy;
— to contribute to sound economic expansion in Member as well as non-member countries in the process of economic development; and
— to contribute to the expansion of world trade on a multilateral, non-discriminatory basis in accordance with international obligations.

The original Member countries of the OECD are Austria, Belgium, Canada, Denmark, France, Germany, Greece, Iceland, Ireland, Italy, Luxembourg, the Netherlands, Norway, Portugal, Spain, Sweden, Switzerland, Turkey, the United Kingdom and the United States. The following countries became Members subsequently through accession at the dates indicated hereafter: Japan (28th April 1964), Finland (28th January 1969), Australia (7th June 1971) and New Zealand (29th May 1973). The Commission of the European Communities takes part in the work of the OECD (Article 13 of the OECD Convention). Yugoslavia takes part in some of the work of the OECD (agreement of 28th October 1961).

The Development Centre of the Organisation for Economic Co-operation and Development was established by decision of the OECD Council on 23rd October 1962.

The purpose of the Centre is to bring together the knowledge and experience available in Member countries of both economic development and the formulation and execution of general economic policies; to adapt such knowledge and experience to the actual needs of countries or regions in the process of development and to put the results at the disposal of the countries by appropriate means.

The Centre has a special and autonomous position within the OECD which enables it to enjoy scientific independence in the execution of its task. Nevertheless, the Centre can draw upon the experience and knowledge available in the OECD in the development field.

Publié en français sous le titre :

LE SECTEUR INFORMEL
DANS LES ANNÉES 80 ET 90

 THE OPINIONS EXPRESSED AND ARGUMENTS EMPLOYED
IN THIS PUBLICATION ARE THE RESPONSIBILITY OF THE AUTHOR AND
DO NOT NECESSARILY REPRESENT THOSE OF THE OECD

*
* *

This study was undertaken in the context of the Development Centre's programme on Employment Policies.

ALSO AVAILABLE

Development Centre Seminars

Restoring Financial Flows to Latin America *edited by Louis Emmerij, Enrique Iglesias* (1991)
(41 91 06 1) ISBN 92-64-13476-X   FF95 £ 11.00   US$20.00   DM37

The Informal Sector Revisited *edited by David Turnham, Bernard Salomé, Antoine Schwarz*
(1990)
(41 90 03 1) ISBN 92-64-13328-3   FF130 £ 16.00   US$28.00   DM51

Fighting Urban Unemployment in Developing Countries (1989)
(41 88 06 1) ISBN 92-64-13125-6   FF190 £ 23.00   US$40.00   DM78

Development Centre Studies

The Tying of Aid (1991)
(41 91 02 1) ISBN 92-64-13459-X   FF60   £ 7.00   US$12.00   DM23

Building Industrial Competitiveness in Developing Countries *by Sanjaya Lall* (1990)
(41 90 07 1) ISBN 92-64-13397-6   FF90   £ 11.00   US$19.00   DM35

Prices charged at the OECD Bookshop.

*THE OECD CATALOGUE OF PUBLICATIONS and supplements will be sent free of charge
on request addressed either to OECD Publications Service,
2, rue André-Pascal, 75775 PARIS CEDEX 16, or to the OECD Distributor in your country.*

TABLE OF CONTENTS

Chapter 1

DEFINITIONS OF THE INFORMAL SECTOR

Chapter 2

INFORMAL SECTOR SURVEY RESULTS: ARTISANS, VENDORS, SUBCONTRACTORS AND UNREGULATED WORKERS

Chapter 3

POLICIES FOR THE INFORMAL SECTOR

ACKNOWLEDGEMENTS

The author would like to thank a number of individuals who provided information and ideas that have been incorporated into the present report, among them Michael Farbman and Fred O'Regan of the US Agency for International Development in Washington, D.C., Victor Tokman, A.S. Bhalla, S.V. Sethuraman and Carlos Maldonado of the International Labour Office in Geneva, Jacques Delons in Buenos Aires, Carl Liedholm and Donald Mead of Michigan State University in East Lansing, and the late Georges Nihan (1936-1979) whose enthousiasm for the informal sector was unbounded.

PREFACE

The review of two decades of informal sector definitions, surveys, policies and programmes presented here reflects my own and the Development Centre's continued concern with the related problems of employment creation and small micro-scale enterprise development. Harold Lubell's monograph follows on the publication of the papers and discussions of the Development Centre's 1988 seminar on *The Informal Sector Revisited* and leads into the work on the informal sector foreseen in the Governance and Entrepreneurship component of the Development Centre's Research Programme for 1990-1992.

The urban informal sector has two important economic and social functions: it produces goods and services that constitute a good part of the consumption baskets of the Third World's poorer consumers; and it absorbs a good proportion of the Third World's urban labour force. It also serves as a major point of entry into urban life and work for a considerable share of rural migrants to the cities. Support to informal sector activity has therefore been seen as an instrument for employment creation and poverty alleviation. More recently the focus has shifted to enhancing the informal sector's potential contribution to economic recovery and development by easing or eliminating regulatory constraints on micro and small scale enterprise activity, which is a variant of the same theme.

Initial expectations that the informal sector would soon be absorbed into the formal have given way to the realization that the informal sector is here to stay, at least through the decade of the 1990s, and the informality even seems to be spreading. The final chapter of this report examines some of the implications.

As manager of the ILO research project on urbanization and employment in developing countries in the 1970s, Harold Lubell was among the ILO's World Employment Programme staff who worked on the urban informal sector after the ILO introduced the concept into general currency. He also brings to the report presented here many years of field experience as a development economist, with the Ford Foundation in Vietnam and Malaysia and with the US Agency for International Development in Turkey, India, Egypt and most recently Senegal. The views he presents are his own and do not necessarily reflect those of the Development Centre.

Louis Emmerij
President of the OECD Development Centre
December 1990

EXECUTIVE SUMMARY

A. Issues

The slowdown of economic growth in the Third World during the 1980s has stimulated renewed interest in the role of the informal sector as producer of goods and services, as sponge for absorbing the otherwise unemployed, and as contributor to the alleviation of poverty. The report presented here reviews a large number of studies carried out since the early 1970s that throw light on the behaviour of informal sector enterprises. The continuing assumption has been that knowledge of informal sector behaviour will improve the design of programmes and projects for support to productive informal sector activities, although there also has always been a lingering doubt as to whether informal sector participants may not prefer official invisibility to possible assistance. The question of income levels of informal sector participants has been an issue in discussions of poverty and of labour market behaviour. An aspect of informal sector behaviour that has come into recent prominence, the informal sector's avoidance of regulations, has raised the issue of how to eliminate unnecessary or counter-productive regulations and the parallel issue of how to reconcile the interests of informal sector producers and those of the community where they are in conflict.

B. Definitions of the Informal Sector

After many years of controversy concerning the nature of informality, the frontier between formality and informality, and the homogeneity or heterogeneity of the informal sector, two characteristics have emerged as operational criteria for identifying informal sector enterprises: small size (micro-scale); and the extent to which an enterprise avoids official regulations and taxes. Within those criteria, exact definitions vary. As discussed in Chapter 1, micro-enterprises have been defined for survey purposes sometimes as enterprises with less than five workers, sometimes less than ten, sometimes less than twenty. Sometimes household servants are included as informals but most often they are not. Often the investigator identifies informality by the outward characteristics of the enterprise, according to Hans Singer's dictum that an informal sector entity is hard to describe but you know it when you see it: the informal sector enterprise is not only small, it is also likely to be located in a dilapidated structure (thus excluding from the informal category most self-employed doctors, lawyers and other liberal professionals whose productive activity is likely to be well-housed).

Avoidance of regulation often goes with micro-size. Staying small contributes to official invisibility and thus to the ability to avoid expense-incurring regulations, but it also has its costs. Recently increased interest in the regulation framework derives from the restrictive effect of unnecessary or counter-productive regulations on micro and small enterprise activity. However, some investigators choose to extend the definition of informality to medium and large scale enterprises that also avoid regulations. In the case of direct evasion where regulations are legitimate, the wider definition fails to distinguish between illegality and informality. In the case of indirect evasion through sub-contracting to successively smaller enterprises, illegality and informality converge.

C. Informal Sector Behaviour

Research on informal sector behaviour, described in Chapter 2, has included analysis of population censuses to estimate the share of informal sector participants in the labour force, direct mini-censuses of informal sector activity in numerous cities, and a considerable number of sample surveys, most of which have dealt with goods production and service activities that offer an evident potential for growth, since it is such activities that policy practitioners believe can be affected by negative or positive interventions from outside the informal sector itself. In particular, most of the work on the informal sector in Africa carried out by the ILO, the World Bank and USAID has looked at goods production and services, branches of activity where injections of credit, training, new technology and technical assistance can help increase productivity, output and incomes. The multitude of petty traders has been the subject of some research but they scarcely appear in discussions of direct assistance. In Asia, informal sector goods production has been the main focus of concern, although there have been some outstanding studies on street traders and hawkers. Researchers in Latin America also have been interested mainly in goods production activities including housing, with recent emphasis on the increasing extent of subcontracting relationships between formal and informal sector producers in the newly industrializing countries. There also have been some studies on the competitive and complementary relationships between formal and informal retail traders, the most significant being for Santiago (Chile). Informal sector urban transport has been a concern of research and regulatory policy in urban Latin America and in the crowded cities of Asia. Domestic service, which is included among informal sector activities in PREALC's definition, has no role for policy since it is expected to disappear as development creates alternative income earning activities for women.

The boundary between the formal and informal sectors has become somewhat fluid as survey information on the informal sector has accumulated, and the heterogeneity of activities within the informal sector in given city and country situations has become evident. Each branch of informal sector activity has specific characteristics resulting from its local technological and social context. Differences between countries and between continents result from differences in levels of industrialization and differences in social structures. Subcontracting from formal sector enterprises to informal sector producers is prevalent in the industrial cities of Mexico and Argentina, but not in much of Sub-Saharan Africa where the small industrial formal sector has been shrinking because of the general economic crisis of the 1980s. Differences in the extent of restrictions on informal sector activity result from differences in the legal and regulatory framework: restrictions are severe in Peru and in other Latin American countries that have retained the traditions and influences of imperial Spain, but they are moderate in francophone Africa and practically non-existent in Nigeria and some other countries of anglophone Africa.

Estimates of incomes in informal sector activities have consistently shown that average earnings of informal sector enterprise heads are higher (and sometimes considerably higher) than the official minimum wage or than the average wage in the formal sector. Higher earnings and an almost universal taste for relative independence explain the positive appeal of informal sector activity to its participants. The evidence on the relation between average wages in the informal and the formal sectors is mixed: wages of hired workers (*i.e.* excluding apprentices) in the informal sector are usually lower than in the formal sector but the reverse is sometimes the case. Nevertheless, informal sector participants usually constitute the bulk of the urban working poor, so that informal sector activity is sometimes a channel for upward mobility but often a last resort for urban survival.

Women of the informal sector are concentrated in petty retail trade, dressmaking, hairdressing and street food preparation. They are usually the poorest among informal sector participants, with some striking exceptions that include the "Mama's Benz" of coastal West Africa who have broken away to become rich as wholesale traders of textiles for women's outerwear.

As discussed in Chapter 5 on special aspects of informality, informal sector participants usually do not have access to formal credit from banks and other institutions. However, large volumes of cash flow into the informal financial market through tontines and other forms of informal group saving. The savings are used mostly for ceremonial and other consumption purposes but they have a considerable potential as a base for credit for working capital and investment.

A significant feature of the informal sector is the importance of the traditional apprenticeship system in transmitting skills to new entrants to the labour force, many of whom receive no other education or training, and in socializing teenage youths. The World Bank, the ILO, and the OECD Development Centre are currently implementing a joint research project on Education and Training for Skills and Income in the Informal Sector in Francophone Africa which is generating new information on apprenticeship arrangements and their impacts.

D. Micro-Enterprise Support Programmes

Most informal sector support programmes have taken the form of credit programmes for micro-enterprises, often supplemented by management assistance, product and technical advice, and training. Chapter 4 describes a selection of such programmes, most of them supported by the aid donors. The most recent evaluations have come to the conclusion that "minimalist" programmes limited to the issue of small loans have been more efficient than more complex programmes. Cost-effective ways of extending technical assistance to the mass of informal sector participants have not yet been found.

E. Policy Implications

There is general agreement that the policy environment affects the functioning of the informal sector, but there has been considerable divergence of opinion as to which aspects of policy are most important. As discussed in Chapter 3, the experts at the ILO in Geneva and at the World Bank in Washington were initially concerned mostly with the macro-economic policies that discriminate against small scale activity by providing explicit and implicit subsidies to larger firms through quantitative restrictions on imports, high import tariffs, irrational tariff structures, overvalued exchange rates, exchange controls, administered allocation of foreign exchange, lower than market rates of interest, and administered credit allocation systems. PREALC had those same concerns but also emphasized the lack of growth strategies as the major constraint on transformation of the informal sector and its absorption into the formal sector in Latin America. The neo-Marxist economists saw Third World informality as an irremediable feature of capitalist imperialism that would be changed only by destruction of the world capitalist system. More recently, the regulatory framework has been identified as the centre of the web of policy constraints on informal sector activity.

The wave of structural adjustment programmes of the 1980s eliminated some of the implicit discrimination against informal sector activity exerted by macro-economic policy:

protection for local monopolies was reduced, currencies were devalued in many instances, interest rates for formal sector borrowers have been raised, and some countries now rely on market forces to allocate credit. In some cases, the difficulties faced by less-protected formal sector firms have provided openings in the domestic market for informal sector producers. In other cases, reduced protection against imports has made both informal and formal sector producers vulnerable to intense competition from foreign goods.

The need for growth is keener than ever after the economic stagnation of the 1980s but it is not evident where the resources to fuel growth will come from. It is in that context that the internal catalytic effect of loosening the constraints placed by the regulatory framework on small scale producers finds its macro-economic rationale. The assumption is that the indigenous entrepreneurial energies released by the removal of unnecessary and inhibitory regulations will compensate in part for lack of foreign investment and will in any case make more efficient use of available resources than is now the case.

The areas of policy choice for national governments with respect to the informal sector in the 1990s will include both the macro-economic measures discussed above and micro-level programmes directly supporting informal sector activities. A specific area where policy decisions should be taken is in the formulation of enabling legislation for mutual savings and loan associations of informal sector producers.

Informal sector activities have two sets of implications for the OECD member countries and for the OECD itself. One set refers to aid flows to the developing countries. Informal sector activities in the developing countries can benefit both from direct assistance (e.g. through credit programmes for micro and small scale enterprises) and indirectly from bigger aid operations such as infrastructure projects. Member countries concerned with development of the informal sector in the Third World will have to choose among those and other competing claims on aid resources. The second set of concerns is more inner-directed. Informality through subcontracting is spreading in the advanced industrial countries as well as in the Third World. OECD member countries will have to decide whether to close an eye to avoidance of labour, health and tax regulations by sweatshops in their own countries in order to promote employment, or whether to enforce such regulations to protect the integrity of the social legislation that has been one of the great positive accomplishments of the 20th century.

ABBREVIATIONS

AID	(US) Agency for International Development
ARTEP	Asian Regional Training and Employment Programme
DANIDA	Danish International Development Agency
EEC	European Economic Community
EPOC	Equity Policy Center
FMO	Nederlandse Financierings Maatschappij voor Ontwikkelingslanden (Netherlands Finance Company for Developing Countries)
GTZ	Gesellschaft für Technische Zuzammenarbeit (F.R. of Germany)
IDB	Inter-American Development Bank
IFAD	International Fund for Agricultural Development
ILO	International Labour Office
JASPA	Jobs and Skills Programme for Africa
KFW	Kreditanstalt für Wiederaufbau (F.R. of Germany)
NGO	Non-governmental organization
NORAD	Norvegian Agency for International Development
OECD	Organization for Economic Cooperation and Development
PECTA	Programme des Emplois et des Compétences Techniques pour l'Afrique
PREALC	Programa para el Empleo en America Latina y el Caribe
PVO	Private voluntary organization
RVB	Raad voor de Beroepskeuzevoorlichting (Commission for Vocational Choice Information) (Netherlands)
SENA	Servicio Nacional de Aprendizaje (Colombia)
SIDA	Swedish International Development Agency
UNDP	United Nations Development Programme
UNIDO	United Nations Industrial Development Organization
USAID	United States Agency for International Development

Chapter 1

DEFINITIONS OF THE INFORMAL SECTOR

Since the ILO Employment Mission to Kenya introduced the concept of the informal sector into international usage in 1972, a number of definitions have been introduced into the literature, the alternatives depending in part on the policy concerns of the various authors. This chapter presents first a small sample of alternative theoretical definitions that have been proposed and then some of the variations that have been introduced when trying to identify informal sector activities in practice.

A. Defining the Informal Sector

The ILO Kenya Mission report defined economic informality as a "way of doing things, characterised by: a) ease of entry; b) reliance on indigenous resources; c) family ownership of resources; d) small scale of operation; e) labour-intensive and adapted technology; f) skills acquired outside the formal school system; and g) unregulated and competitive markets"[1]. Subsequent research has shown that some of the listed characteristics should be qualified with the adverb "relatively": e.g. it turns out that in many instances entry is not especially easy, that resource inputs are often of foreign origin, and that markets are unregulated only because the enterprises either are ignorant of existing government regulations or consciously evade government attempts to impose them. Nevertheless, most subsequent definitions have been only variants of the Kenya report's list, with different internal emphases.

S.V. Sethuraman[2] used an establishment or production unit definition of informality. Sethuraman pointed out that the multiplicity of criteria in the definition of informality proposed by the ILO Kenya report caused ambiguity because each criterion could be used to create a universe of its own; he therefore proposed a general definition of the informal sector as small-scale units engaged in the production and distribution of goods and services whose primary objective was to generate employment for the participants rather than to maximise profits.

The ILO/PREALC studies on the informal sector in Latin America and the Caribbean used two alternative definitions of informal sector activity. The first, based on labour force status, included the following: domestic servants; casual workers; own-account workers; and persons working in enterprises of less than five persons (enterprise heads, white-collar employees, blue-collar workers, and family workers). The other definition used an income

17

criterion: persons earning less than a certain minimum, usually the legal minimum wage, "on the assumption that low-productivity activities typical of the informal sector also generate low incomes"[3].

Dipak Mazumdar, in his work for the World Bank, looked at informality as a labour market phenomenon that could explain difference in incomes at the lower end of the income distribution[4]. The informals were those working in activities "unprotected" by company policy, government regulations, or trade union action. An historical example of informality in a dual labour market cited by Mazumdar was the pool of casual day labourers available to the Bombay textile industry to supplement a stable core of relatively high-paid permanent workers who constituted the formal labour force. Wages of the permanent workers were higher than those paid to the day labourers; because the companies restricted entry to the "protected" pool of permanent workers, the informals were unable to bid down wages of the permanent workers. Today the permanent workers are protected by their trade unions and have access to social benefits; the casual day labourers are still unprotected.

A number of recent studies, mostly concerned with Latin America but extending to the developed countries as well, have identified informality with illegality: illegal in the sense that informal activities do not comply with regulations pertaining to fiscal, employment, health and other matters because of flaws in the tax system and in other laws and regulations. The most prominent proponent of the illegality position is Hernando de Soto[5] but it has now been adopted by a number of other analysts as well. It has been pointed out, however, that although a considerable number of legal provisions may weigh upon the informal sector, the actual degree of regulation may be low if the regulations are not strictly applied so that "what is theoretically illegal may well constitute everyday practice"[6]. Unfortunately, the existence of unenforced regulations leaves the informal sector open to harassment and racketeering by the police.

Jacques Charmes[7] has pointed out that the ILO Kenya Mission report's conception of the informal sector contained two elements: marginality and productive activity. Some academic research focused on marginality: activities such as street hawking, garbage picking, and casual labour. The ILO studies, and particularly George Nihan's surveys of the "modern" informal sector in francophone Africa summarised in Chapter 2 below, focused on the productive accomplishments and potentialities of micro-enterprises. Philippe Hugon[8] and some of the British economists[9] also focused on the petty producer (*petit producteur marchand*) component of the informal sector but with a "radical" bias. They consider the situation of the petty producers as part of the working poor to be the result of a capitalist plot to perpetuate a reserve army of labour and to lower the cost of wage-goods of workers in the formal sector in order to reduce wages in the formal (capitalist) sector.

Indian statisticians often use non-registration under the Shops and Establishments Act as one of the key criteria for defining informal sector activity. The Statistics Department of the ILO has been trying for several years to obtain agreement on a statistical definition of the informal sector for measurement purposes. Their 1987 proposal, presented to the 14th International Conference of Labour Statisticians[10], suggested defining the informal sector to include those working during the reference week in an unregistered economic unit or in a registered economic unit having characteristics (level of organisation, scale of operation, and level of technology) similar to unregistered units in the corresponding branch of economic activity.

18

B. Identifying Informal Sector Activities and Participants

Where informal sector participants are identified through a household sample survey, the universe is the households of the geographical area concerned. A sub-sample of informals can be identified by their characteristics which can be either their labour force status (not covered by social security or other labour regulations) or the type of work they do and the nature of the establishment in which they work. Identifying informal sector participants through an establishment survey can involve two steps: deciding a) which units to cover in a survey if the definition of informality contains some degree of ambiguity, and b) which of the units picked up in a survey to label as informal.

Sethuraman's proposed key for identifying informal sector activity was a) all enterprises or production units with less than a maximum number of workers (usually ten) or b) an enterprise with more than the suggested maximum number of workers that satisfied at least one of the following additional criteria: it operated illegally; it worked on an irregular basis; it was located in a temporary structure or in the open; it did not use electric power; it did not depend on formal credit institutions; it did not rely on a formal distribution network; most of its workers had less than six years of schooling. Other criteria could be added according to the preferences of the researcher.

In practice, when establishment surveys are used to examine the characteristics and performance of the informal sector, size of establishment is the indicator most frequently used. There is, however, considerable variation from one survey to another in the size chosen as the cut-off point. As will be noted in Chapter 2 below, the cut-off point is sometimes 5, sometimes 10, sometimes 20; sometimes the number refers to the enterprise head and paid employees without regard to the number of unpaid family workers and apprentices working in the enterprise. Another frequently used indicator is the physical appearance of the enterprise and the kind of structure (or non-structure) in which it operates: the enterprise is considered to be informal for the purposes of the survey if the structure that houses it looks temporary, or is made of scrap or non-permanent materials, if it works in somebody's backyard or basement or in front of a dwelling or in the open under a tree or by the roadside or on the street. The most telling description of the process of identifying an informal sector enterprise was Hans Singer's *bon mot*: "An informal sector enterprise is like a giraffe; it's hard to describe but you know one when you see one".

Notes and References

1. ILO (1972).
2. SETHURAMAN (1981a) and SETHURAMAN (1981b).
3. SOUZA and TOKMAN (1976).
4. MAZUMDAR (1976).
5. DE SOTO (1989).
6. GUERGUIL (1988).
7. CHARMES (1990).
8. HUGON *et al.* (1977).
9. BROMLEY (1979).
10. ILO (1987).

Chapter 2

INFORMAL SECTOR SURVEY RESULTS: ARTISANS, VENDORS, SUBCONTRACTORS AND UNREGULATED WORKERS

The behaviour of informal sector participants has been examined in a considerable number of surveys since the Kenya report of the ILO's World Employment Program focused international attention on the informal sector in 1972[1]. This chapter attempts to summarise the findings of a large sample of informal sector studies carried out since then under the auspices of the ILO and a variety of other international, governmental, academic, and other organisations.

Research on the informal sector has flourished in countries on all three continents of the developing world, but more prominently in Africa and Latin America than in Asia. The surveys discussed below were of three types. The first dealt with the informal sector as a labour force phenomenon, a sector where a good share of the poorer urban working population of the developing countries is employed outside of regular formal sector jobs that carry with them access to social security and other fringe benefits. The concern of such studies was primarily to identify the working poor, to legitimise informal sector occupations in the eyes of usually hostile governments, and to set a framework for marcoeconomic policies that would improve the productivity and incomes of informal sector participants or lead to the latter's absorption into the formal sector. The second deals with the presumably "viable" components of the informal sector as micro-enterprises whose dynamism can be enhanced by judicious injections of funding and technical assistance. The third is a more recent variant of the labour force approach that looks at the growing linkages between formality and informality in the newly industrialising countries, particularly in Latin America where a system of cascading subcontracting from large firms to small firms to basement workshops and to household workers appears to be in full development.

The African informal sector studies quickly went beyond the initial labour force approach to examine the micro-enterprise as a production entity. The Asian studies followed the same pattern. Most of the earlier Latin American studies used the labour force approach since their concern was employment policy. Later the Latin American studies took several tracks. The labour force approach in Latin America developed into an examination of the regulated or unregulated status of workers in enterprises of all sizes and degrees of visibility or clandestinity. The enterprise approach split into examinations of competitivity between informal and formal enterprises (one of Victor Tokman's concerns) and of the role of the regulatory superstructure in hampering growth of small-scale private enterprises (the Hernando de Soto approach).

21

A. Africa

1. The ILO Kenya Employment Mission Report

The ILO Kenya Employment Mission Report[1] estimated the size of the urban informal sector in 1969 in all of Kenya at around 100 000 out of an urban African working population in the neighbourhood of 410 000. The 100 000 included 32 000 in Nairobi, 44 000 in Mombasa and 24 000 in smaller towns of Kenya. Specification of the categories of informal sector activities in the report is rather impressionistic. The text makes the point that employed in the informal sector are "a variety of carpenters, masons, tailors and other tradesmen, as well as cooks and taxi-drivers" in addition to the "petty traders, street hawkers, shoeshine boys and other groups 'underemployed' on the streets of the big towns" (p. 5) as well as women involved in informal activities such as illegal beer brewing, prostitution, urban agriculture and homecraft production "that are difficult to cover statistically" (pp. 54, 343). The ILO Kenya mission's estimate of the number of informal sector participants in Nairobi was derived separately for squatter settlements and non-squatter settlements from the estimated African population of Nairobi on the basis of the number of establishments in five categories of activity per thousand of population as estimated in the University of Nairobi's 1969 Methare Valley survey. The five categories were: general stores; cafés or hotels; other retail trade; artisans; and other activities (p. 342). The point the report wanted to make concerning the informal sector was that its activities were "economically efficient and profit-making though small in scale and limited by simple technologies, little capital and lack of links with the formal sector" and that they offered "virtually the full range of basic skills needed to provide goods and services for a large though often poor section of the population" (p. 5).

2. ILO Urbanisation and Employment Research Project Studies

Following up the ILO Kenya Employment Mission Report's identification of the informal sector as a locus of economic dynamism and contributor to economic growth, the ILO World Employment Programme's research programme on urbanisation and employment incorporated the urban informal sector as a major theme of enquiry and analysis. Chapters on the informal sector were included in several of the urbanisation and employment city monographs, in particular the monograph on Abidjan[2], and a dozen special studies were carried out in Africa, Asia and Latin America[3] using, as a common element, a questionnaire designed by S.V. Sethuraman[4].

Among the cities in Africa included in the informal sector studies series were Freetown (Sierra Leone), Kano (Nigeria) and Kumasi (Ghana)[5]. A Marxist view of the informal sector was presented in a World Employment Programme research working paper on Dakar[6].

a. Abidjan (Côte d'Ivoire), 1970

The first quantification of the "informal sector" in Abidjan was derived by Heather Joshi from figures for the "traditional sector" presented in a planning document prepared for the government of Côte d'Ivoire by a French consulting firm, Société d'Etudes Economiques et Financières[2]. Of the estimated 153 000 working population of Abidjan in 1970, 47 000 (31 per cent) were informal, 6 per cent of whom were in agriculture, 32 per cent in industry and construction, 35 per cent in trade and 27 per cent services. The estimates included self-employed, family workers and employees but excluded the market women (*tabliers*). In fact, women constituted over half of the retail traders involved in the selling of food, prepared dishes and beverages which was the focus of a good 40 per cent of all retail trade.

For the Côte d'Ivoire as a whole, value added per worker in the informal sector, where little capital is used, was 23 per cent the level of that in the formal sector in manufacturing and construction, and 24 per cent in transport; however it was 54 per cent in trade and services.

b. Freetown (Sierra Leone), 1976

The survey of the self-employed and micro-enterprise heads carried out in Freetown by D.A. Fowler in 1976 covered activities in goods production (manufacturing), construction, trade, transport and services. Almost two thirds (65 per cent) were in trade (50 per cent in retail trade), 20 per cent were in goods production, 9 per cent in services, 4 per cent in transport, and 2 per cent in construction. Almost a quarter of the sample were women, most of whom were in retail trade but also in food processing, textile production, and restaurant activities. Close to three quarters (74 per cent) of the enterprises were single person activities (own account workers), 10 per cent employed one other worker, 7 per cent employed two other workers, and 9 per cent employed three or more. Average size of enterprise in terms of number of persons was 1.9. In trade, 84 per cent of the enterprises consisted of own-account workers with no employees; in goods production and in transport the figure was 54 per cent; in construction, it was 30 per cent. Only 57 per cent of employees were paid; the remaining 43 per cent were family workers or apprentices.

Over 70 per cent of the self-employed and micro-enterprise heads had no education at all, about 20 per cent had some primary-level education, and about 10 per cent had some secondary-level education or more. The level of education was correlated with age since many of the younger self-employed had migrated into Freetown from places where access to education was less available than in Freetown: rural areas of Sierra Leone or other countries. The bulk (92 per cent) of male entrepreneurs who had never attended school were migrants into Freetown.

Of the sample 54 per cent acquired their skills as apprentices before establishing their businesses, 40 per cent (mostly in trade) on the job, and 1 per cent by attending training institutions while the other 5 per cent were self-taught. Half of those who had attended a training institution acquired further training on the job. Most of the secondary school dropouts subsequently went through a period of apprenticeship.

Estimated average net revenue of all the individuals in the sample was below the legal minimum wage, but it was well above the legal minimum wage in construction and transport. Within manufacturing, average net revenue was well above the legal minimum wage in food processing, textiles, and woodworking and furniture making; average net revenue was particularly low in leatherworking and footwear.

The average wage paid to wage-workers by the micro-enterprise heads was below the legal minimum because of a particularly low level of wages in trade, but the average wage of workers in manufacturing activities was close to the legal minimum wage and in construction considerably above it. Apprentices received meals, shelter (except for natives of Freetown), training, and occasionally very small amounts of pocket money. Immigrants from Guinea who joined enterprises of relatives as apprentices often assisted with domestic chores as well.

At least some capital equipment (machines, tools, furniture and fixtures, vehicles) was owned by 80 per cent of the sample of self-employed. Most of the equipment was inexpensive and locally made. Only 3 per cent owned capital equipment worth over $500, mostly in mechanised transport, metal working and services.

Most inputs (backward linkages) were purchased from formal sector enterprises (44 per cent from formal sector retailers). Most sales (forward linkages) were made to individuals and households. Some of the larger of the enterprises in the sample sold to other enterprises.

Only a quarter of the sample indicated that they would prefer wage employment to their present working activity.

c. Lagos (Nigeria), 1976

In the Lagos (Nigeria) informal sector survey carried out by O.J. Fapohunda in 1976, the informal sector was defined as enterprises employing ten workers or less, whose owners did not have more than a school certificate standard of education or access to the formal sector capital market. The sample covered just over 2 000 enterprises, 40 per cent of them in goods production (manufacturing), 31 per cent in trade (including restaurants), 15 per cent in services, 3 per cent in utilities and construction, 4 per cent in transport and 7 per cent in other ill-defined activities. Trade was under-represented in the sample. Only 5 per cent of the sample entrepreneurs came from Lagos state; 87 per cent came from other states of Nigeria and the other 8 per cent from other countries. Of the migrants, 85 per cent came from rural areas. Only 15 per cent of the sample enterprise heads were women because of the under-representation of trade in the sample.

Of the enterprise heads in the Lagos sample, 74 per cent had received some formal education (18 per cent beyond the primary level), 13 per cent had received some informal training on the job in small enterprises or as apprentices, and 11 per cent had received no education or specific training.

Average (mean) earnings of enterprise heads in the Lagos sample were well above the legal minimum wage although the median of earnings was somewhat below it so that more than half of the enterprise heads earned less than the minimum wage. Almost 80 per cent of the enterprise heads were satisfied with their present occupations and were not interested in seeking a job as a wage-earner in the formal sector.

The average size of enterprise was 2.1 persons including the enterprise head. Half of the enterprise heads worked alone, about a quarter were two-person enterprises, and the other quarter were three or more person enterprises. The average level of schooling of the other participants was lower than that of the enterprise heads. Over half of the enterprises used apprentices, three-quarters of whom were unpaid, 15 per cent were paid reduced wages, and 10 per cent were paid full wages. Over half of the apprentices left the enterprise within three or four years, many of them to establish their own enterprises. Payment to apprentices was usually in kind (food and shelter).

Wages paid to employees receiving wages were below (in most cases well below) the legal minimum wage. About a third of the enterprises paid wages on a daily basis, a quarter on a monthly basis, and most of the others irregularly.

Over 90 per cent of the enterprises in the Lagos sample were in fixed locations, two-thirds of them in permanent structures; 61 per cent were located in part of a residential unit. Only a quarter of the enterprises had both water and electricity; 50 per cent had electricity only. Some capital equipment was owned (or to a limited extent rented) by 79 per cent of the enterprises. The average (mean) value of equipment was around $720, but the median value was about $400. The modest value of capital equipment owned and the general practice of renting premises reflected the limited access to capital of the enterprises in the sample. Many of the enterprises also had cash-flow problems since fewer than two-thirds were paid prior to or immediately upon delivery but most of them paid cash for purchased inputs. Only 18 per cent of the sample had ever applied for bank credit and very few of those succeeded in getting any.

Of the customers of the Lagos informal sector enterprises, 87 per cent were households and 9 per cent were other informal sector enterprises. Forward linkages to formal sector enterprises were negligible.

Direct government restrictions did not appear to affect the enterprises in the Lagos sample. Most of them operated without licenses of any kind, only a quarter paid any taxes to the government, and only about 14 per cent were subject to any kind of inspection or regulation. On the other hand, the enterprise heads indicated that they would like government assistance in obtaining credit, market place facilities, and greater access to orders from formal sector businesses and government.

Some 40 per cent of the Lagos enterprise heads had no dependants, but the average size of household for the others was 6.5 persons, 81 per cent of them under the age of 14. About half of the multiple-member households had secondary earners, not all of whom contributed to household expenses.

d. Kano (Nigeria), 1976

The 1976 Kano (Nigeria) informal sector survey by A.L. Mabogunje and M.O. Filani was carried out in two stages: a complete census of enterprises (6 665) in the city, from which was chosen a sample of 505 enterprises employing a total of 903 persons including the enterprise head.

Of the enterprises identified in the census, 60 per cent were in trade. However the sample was biased to focus more on non-trade activities: 71 per cent of the sample enterprises were in manufacturing and technical repair services, 15 per cent were in personal services, and 14 per cent were in trade. Over 80 per cent of the sample enterprises were in three of the eight wards of Kano city, with the largest concentration in the old city which contained two-thirds of the population of metropolitan Kano in 1962. Of the total number of persons employed in the sample enterprises, 63 per cent were heads of enterprise, 21 per cent were journeymen (skilled workers) and 16 per cent were apprentices. Most of the apprentices were below 14 years of age. Women accounted for only 11 per cent of these working in the sample enterprises since Kano, in northern Nigeria, is very much a Moslem city. The women worked mainly in sewing, grain milling and hairdressing. Education levels varied: 12 per cent of the participants had no education at all; 46 per cent had only Arabic training; 12 per cent were below the primary VI level in the English-language system, 26 per cent had attained the primary VI level and 4 per cent had attended secondary school.

The proportion of migrants among the informal sector participants (35 per cent) was slightly higher than that estimated for the population as a whole (20 to 30 per cent). Most of the migrants came from Nigerian states other than Kano. A somewhat higher proportion of migrants (over two-thirds) than of natives (60 per cent) owned their enterprises. Apprentices also accounted for a higher proportion of migrants (19 per cent) than of natives (16 per cent).

Wage-workers (journeymen) accounted for a lower proportion of migrants than of natives. Immigration was recent: two-thirds of the migrants had arrived in Kano during the five years preceding the survey.

Of the enterprise heads, two thirds worked alone. Those who did employ additional workers had on the average one journeyman and one apprentice. In some activities, the number of workers was larger: 5.3 in bakeries, 4 in construction; 3.8 in leather manufacturing; 3.8 in welding; 3 in roadside mechanical and electrical work.

Most of the male enterprise heads in the Kano sample, but considerably fewer of the women, had incomes above the legal minimum wage. However, 36 per cent of all participants reported zero income (including, presumably, many of the apprentices) and 27 per cent received less than the legal minimum wage.

Initial capital outlay in Kano's informal sector enterprises was considerably lower than in Lagos. The average (mean) capital outlay in Kano was $450, compared with $720 in Lagos. The median capital outlay in Kano was only $80. The sources of financing were personal savings (70 per cent), borrowing from friends and relatives (29 per cent), and bank credit (1 per cent). As in Lagos, 87 per cent of sales were to households; 10.5 per cent were to small enterprises. Much of the raw materials and other inputs used originated in the formal sector but passed through retail traders as intermediaries.

Most of the Kano informal sector enterprise heads cited lack of capital as a major constraint on expansion, and access to credit as the most desirable form of government assistance.

e. Kumasi (Ghana), 1975

The 1975 Kumasi (Ghana) informal sector sample survey by George Aryee covered 298 informal sector enterprises in manufacturing other than food processing: 25 per cent in motor repair and maintenance (for which Kumasi is noted), 24 per cent in tailoring and dressmaking, 23 per cent in footwear and leatherware, and the others in metalworking, blacksmithing, carpentry, wood carving, cane weaving, and carpets and doormats. All the entrepreneurs in the sample were males.

A third of the enterprise heads in the Kumasi survey were migrants from outside of the Ashanti region (of which Kumasi is the capital) including 5 per cent from outside of Ghana, 3 per cent were born in Kumasi, and the rest came from other parts of the Ashanti region. The level of education among the enterprise heads was relatively high: 60 per cent had ten years of schooling (middle level education) or more. However, 28 per cent had no formal schooling at all. The level of education among migrants from outside the Ashanti region was lower than for the Ashantis. Over 90 per cent of the enterprise heads had received their technical training as apprentices in the informal sector.

The enterprises in the Kumasi sample were clustered in specific locations within the city where specific activities were specialised, e.g. Suame Magazine for auto repair and related activites, and Angloga for carpentry. Many of the enterprises were housed in temporary structures and most of them lacked minimum support facilities such as water and electricity.

In Suame Magazine, the city council owned the land and collected a token rent from the enterprises installed there, but it forbade construction of permanent structures because the council intended eventually to build permanent workshops.

Of the total of 1 329 persons working in the Kumasi sample of informal sector enterprises, 24 per cent were working proprietors (including partners), 5 per cent were journeymen, 65 per cent were apprentices and 6 per cent were unpaid family workers. Apprentices paid a fee to the enterprise head; in return they received training, food, shelter and small amounts of pocket money. The average (mean) size of enterprise was 4.5 persons. Only 15 per cent of the sample enterprises were single person activities; 47 per cent had 2 to 4 persons working, 31 per cent had 5 to 9, and 7 per cent had 10 or more. In motor repair and maintenance, 78 per cent of the enterprises had 5 or more persons working, most of them apprentices.

The average (mean) amount of fixed capital per enterprise was $680; the median was $330. The capital to labour ratio was correspondingly low.

Average (mean) earnings of the enterprise heads in the Kumasi sample were around $68 per week, with the median at $35 per week, compared with the legal minimum wage of some $13 per week. The earnings of the enterprise head increased with size of enterprise, *i.e.* with the number of apprentices.

Most of the enterprises in the Kumasi sample purchased their inputs from retailers. Backward linkages to the formal sector were therefore indirect except for some of the larger enterprises. Over 72 per cent of the enterprises sold their output mainly to households; virtually none sold directly to the formal sector.

f. Dakar (Senegal), 1974: A Marxist View

Chris Gerry's 1974 study of Dakar's informal sector[6] included: a) A survey (using a questionnaire based on Sethuraman's) of 285 artisans and "petty producers" in four groups of activities: carpenters and furniture makers; shoemakers, shoe repairers, and other leather and plastic workers; tailors, embroiderers and related activities; vehicle repairers, metalworkers and related activities; b) A survey (using a short questionnaire) of 100 casual (temporary) workers; c) Interviews with 80 producers and traders in a poor but active section of Dakar; d) An examination of recycling ("recuperative") activities; and e) A look at illegal activities such as smuggling, selling of illegal alcoholic beverages and prostitution.

Gerry distinguished between petty producers and artisans. Petty producers were identified by Karl Marx as pre-capitalist small-scale producers for the market. Artisans were defined by Gerry as producers for sale to an individual customer on demand. The transition from artisan (in Gerry's sense) to petty producer implied increased capital investment ("accumulation of capital") and some use of wage labour to supplement the labour inputs of family workers, apprentices, and the artisan himself. Few of the enterprises Gerry surveyed in Dakar had made that transition.

Gerry dealt with the linkages between petty producers including artisans (the informal sector) and the modern capitalist economy (the formal sector) first by looking into the sources of raw materials used by informal sector producers. Gerry noted that except for shoemaking and some artistic handicrafts, most petty producers relied on goods originating directly or indirectly from outside of Senegal, either imported for direct use or produced locally from imported spare parts and raw materials. Metalworkers using iron and steel, and producing mainly window frames, wrought iron gates and grills, and beds, had input linkages to large industrial and commercial firms and were dependent on commercial importers for cutting and welding gases. Practically all the cloth brought to artisan tailors by individual customers was either directly imported or produced locally by formal sector producers (identified disparagingly by Gerry as "largely foreign-owned or foreign-controlled").

Plastic workers used plastic materials imported by Lebanese commercial enterprises. Over three-quarters of the furniture makers obtained their raw materials from large suppliers. The shoemakers used leather from BATA for fancy footwear; otherwise they relied on artisanally tanned leather treated by Mauritanian women in an open space between the central and peripheral wards of Pikine (Dakar's major shanty town suburban section) close to the slaughterhouses. The Mauritanian women also occasionally purchased reptile skins brought to Dakar from Sine-Saloum. (It would be interesting to find out what has happened to artisanal leather tanning in Dakar since the 1988 expulsion and exodus of Mauritanians from Senegal). Many of the artisanal leather workers were Sarakole (Soninke) dry-season immigrants to the Rebeuss section of Dakar from the Senegal River region of eastern Senegal and western Mali; the majority of the leather workers using reptile skins were concentrated in central Pikine. On the sales side, according to Gerry, "the majority of petty producers are not integrated into [wholesale and retail] commercial networks, but generate most of their income through personal artisan-client relationships, furnishing articles for immediate consumption, with no commercial mediation" (p. 60).

Gerry's review of skills acquisition by Dakar's informal sector sample of 285 petty producers and artisans showed that 67 per cent had been apprentices to artisans, small producers or small self-employed jobbing sub-contractors (tacherons), 21 per cent had worked as employees or apprentices in small enterprises, and only 12 per cent had received their training in a formal technical school, in the army, in one or another of the state organisations such as the Public Works Department, or in a large foreign enterprise based in Dakar. However, except for shoemakers and leather workers, a considerable proportion of petty producers and artisans had had considerable experience as wage-workers, as indicated below (in per cent):

Occupational category	Proportion of sample with wage-work experience	Average (mean) proportion of work-life spent in spent in wage-work	Median proportion of work-life spent in wage-work
Furniture makers	70.5	51.0	55.0
Shoemakers and leather workers	9.5	47.5	58.5
Tailors	21.1	8.6	65.0
Mechanics and related	54.8	53.7	55.0

The shift out of wage employment in the early 1970s was probably due mostly to a reduction of activity in formal sector manufacturing.

3. ILO Francophone Africa Urban Informal Sector Research Project Surveys

Surveys were carried out under the supervision of Georges Nihan during the period 1977-79 for the ILO research programme on skills acquisition and self-employment in the urban informal sector of francophone Africa in Nouakchott (Mauritania)[7], Lomé (Togo)[8], Bamako (Mali)[9], Kigali (Rwanda)[10] and Yaoundé (Cameroun)[11]. A decade later, USAID/Senegal used Nihan's framework as the basis for a similar survey in Dakar (Senegal)[12]. The purpose of the ILO programme was to investigate the training and employment potential of the "modern" informal sector activities in manufacturing, services and construction that looked as if they could be expanded if they received appropriate assistance.

a. Nouakchott (Mauritania), 1977

The pioneering survey in the series launched by Georges Nihan was done in Nouakchott (Mauritania) in 1977[7]. An informal sector census was carried out in the city by the ILO team covering non-itinerant activities, including market-place commerce but not off-market commerce. The census estimated a total of 2 936 informal sector enterprises including an enumerated 1 016 petty traders and an estimated 1 000 off-market traders, and an identified 920 in production (421 in manufacturing, 405 in services, and 94 in construction). The follow-up survey covered 323 enterprises in manufacturing (excluding tailors and some other trades), services and construction.

The manufacturing, services and construction group employed an average of 4.8 persons per enterprise, one-third of them apprentices, in addition to the enterprise head. Adding partners and assuming total employment in petty trade at 1.5 times the number of traders noted above (our assumption, not Nihan's), total employment in the informal sector of Nouakchott would have come to around 8 400 of the 70 000 in Nouakchott's working age population. Modern sector employment came to 5 500 throughout the country.

Aside from the apprentices and some family helpers and day-labourers, wages paid were at the same level as in the formal sector. The enterprise heads earned two or three times the official minimum wage for a skilled worker.

The main source of training in Nouakchott's informal sector (manufacturing and services) was apprenticeship: 41.6 per cent of the work-force in manufacturing consisted of apprentices and 63.5 per cent in services, although in construction only 3.7 per cent were apprentices. Apprentices received payment (in cash and in kind) equivalent of an unskilled labourer. Of the informal sector entrepreneurs, 64.3 per cent in manufacturing, 84.2 per cent in services and 21.6 per cent in construction had received their training in the informal sector; 53 per cent of the entrepreneurs in the sample had not attended primary school and 55 per cent came from a traditional background in agriculture, animal husbandry or fishing.

Nihan was surprised by the high value of machinery and equipment he found in many of the ramshackle structures which served as workplaces for the informal sector of Nouakchott. For the upper tenth of the sample, gross fixed assets averaged around $27 400 in manufacturing, $24 980 in services and $62 000 in construction; half of the entrepreneurs had assets of at least $450 in manufacturing, $500 in services and $2 700 in construction. The cost of equipment per job in the sample enterprises was barely 5 per cent of that in the formal sector, while labour productivity was about 30 per cent of that in the formal sector.

b. Lomé (Togo), 1977

The 1977 Lomé (Togo) survey also began with an exhaustive census of the informal sector including commerce. The census was followed up by a sample survey of the categories of "modern" informal sector activities thought to be the most dynamic: woodworking, metalworking, construction, and mechanical and electrical repairs.

The census enumerated a total of 23 824 informal sector economic units in Lomé of which 1 863 were in the "modern" informal sector group, 18 975 were in commerce and the remaining 2 886 were in other activities. The follow-up survey covered 280 of the 1 863 enterprises in the "modern" informal sector group.

On the basis of the survey, it was estimated that the "modern" informal sector group employed a total work-force of 6 091, including 3 586 apprentices, 483 wage-earning journeymen, and 87 working partners in addition to the 1 863 enterprise heads. Employment in the formal sector in all of Togo came to about 12 000 in 1977. The bulk (73 per cent) of the entrepreneurs earned more than they would have as wage-earners in the formal sector and 83 earned incomes equal to or greater than the guaranteed inter-occupational minimum wage (SMIG) as did 69 per cent of the journeymen wage-earners. Of the entrepreneurs, 96 per cent had received their own training as apprentices in the informal sector. Apprentice training serves both as preparation for self-employment and for employment in the modern formal sector where many apprentices do find jobs at some point in their working lives.

Technical management and accounting skills were in short supply among the entrepreneurs in the Lomé sample: only 21 per cent kept a record of receipts and expenditures, and only 2.5 per cent kept more sophisticated accounts. Only 2 per cent of the entrepreneurs took account of depreciation in calculating their production costs.

Educational levels were low. Of the informal sector entrepreneurs, 25 per cent were illiterate, 19 per cent had at most three years of primary schooling and 5 per cent had attended secondary school. Of the apprentices, 36 per cent were illiterate.

The entrepreneurs in the Lomé sample were highly suspicious of government institutions. They were overwhelmingly in favour of setting up a mutual aid association run by the entrepreneurs themselves.

c. Kigali (Rwanda), 1977

The 1977 ILO census of the informal sector of Kigali was limited to two sections of the city where most of the "modern" informal sector activities were concentrated: Biryogo for production and services and Gikondo for construction. In Biryogo, which has a population of 7 500, 308 informal sector units were identified, 52 per cent of them in commerce. They employed a total of 711 persons including the enterprise heads. The primary criterion of identification was visual: the type of structure sheltering the workplace. In Gikondo, 22 construction material enterprises were identified out of a total of 124. The follow-up survey covered 11 of the construction material (brick-making) enterprises in Gikondo and 37 of the production and services enterprises in Biryogo.

The role of the apprenticeship system was considerably less important in Kigali than in the other cities investigated. The only activity where apprentices formed a significant part of the work-force was woodworking where apprentices accounted for 25 per cent of the work-force but only 10 out of 25 (40 per cent) of the woodworking enterprises employed apprentices. Of the 10, only 7 entrepreneurs systematically provided training to their apprentices. The rate of literacy (82 per cent) among the apprentices in Kigali was higher than in most of the other African cities where surveys have been carried out.

The average value of the capital stock of the enterprises covered was about $1 450 ($6 190 for the top decile). Financing of the capital investment was largely endogenous to the informal sector enterprises themselves. The average income derived by the entrepreneurs in woodworking was the equivalent of a fairly highly paid worker in a large-scale formal sector enterprise; in the other sub-branches of activity, average earnings were close to the level of an unskilled worker in the formal sector.

d. Bamako (Mali), 1978

The ILO's 1978 Bamako (Mali) informal sector census, which excluded itinerant vendors, enumerated a total of 16 859 enterprises, 67 per cent of them in fixed-location commerce, 24 per cent in production (10 per cent in tailoring), 8 per cent in services (2 per cent in laundering and dry cleaning), and 1 per cent in construction. The centre of the city (Koulouba Centre Commercial) and two semi-peripheral wards (Hamdalaye and Misira N'Gomi) contained half of the enumerated activities. The "modern" informal sector component consisted of a total of 1 160 enterprises: 394 (34 per cent) in production (excluding tailoring, watch repairs and certain other activities), 577 (50 per cent) in services, and 189 (16 per cent) in construction. The follow-up survey covered 226 of the 1 160 enterprises defined as the "modern" informal sector of Bamako.

On the basis of the Bamako survey, it was estimated that the 1 160 enterprises employed 1 426 wage-workers, partners, and paid family workers and around 1 900 apprentices for a total of 4 486 including the enterprise heads themselves. The enterprise heads reported spending an average of 5.8 hours per week (10 per cent of their work time) training their apprentices. The survey results indicated that 80 per cent of the apprentices received payment (in cash and in kind) on average equivalent to 49 per cent of the SMIG. The bulk (76 per cent) of the enterprise heads had received their own training as apprentices in the informal sector.

According to the Bamako survey, 90 per cent of the enterprise heads in the "modern" informal sector derived incomes equal to or greater than the SMIG; 50 per cent of them earned at least an amount four times the SMIG. Of the wage-workers, 79 per cent were paid more than the SMIG. Capital per enterprise was low: 66 per cent of the enterprises had capital valued at $216 or less. The top 6 per cent had capital valued at over $2 150 per enterprise; for them, the average was $4 300. Financing for capital investment was largely internally generated: 77 per cent of the artisans in the sample had financed their equipment purchases out of their own resources, as did 95 per cent of those who had enlarged their workshops.

Forward linkages (sales) of the informal sector to the formal sector were weak: 53 per cent of sales were made to the poor of Bamako and to other artisans and small traders, 30 per cent to government officials, and 17 per cent to formal sector commerce, modern sector enterprises and the government.

The level of management accounting was extremely low among the Bamako informal sector entrepreneurs: 3 per cent kept a record of receipts and expenses and another 3 per cent had more sophisticated accounts. For setting prices, 78 per cent reported that the basis was bargaining with the customer while 7 per cent claimed that they calculated their cost-price (and only 1 per cent could do so correctly). However, only 31 per cent of the entrepreneurs in the sample expressed any interest in improving their accounting skills.

The types of assistance desired by the Bamako informal sector entrepreneurs were technical training (70 per cent) and management training (64 per cent), preferably individualised and provided at the workplace. Only 13 per cent were interested in training provided in a centre established by the government; a minority (37 per) cent were willing to accept assistance provided through a co-operative. However, 67 per cent were interested in a mutual aid association provided it was organised and managed by themselves. The entrepreneurs' reaction to the possibility of granting their apprentices permission to participate for several hours during the week in an outside training course was largely negative: 44 per cent stated that they were opposed.

e. Yaoundé (Cameroun), 1978

The ILO's 1978 census of the informal sector of Yaoundé (Cameroun) covered all economic activities except construction and transport. The follow-up survey covered a sample of the informal sector activities defined by Nihan as "modern": production (woodworking and metalworking); services (mechanical and electrical repairs and small-scale engineering); and clothing (tailoring and leatherworking). The census enumerated 15 364 enterprises of which 80 per cent were in commerce; the "modern" group included 2 596 entrepreneurs working with 146 partners, 172 paid family workers, 549 wage employees, and 3 342 apprentices for total employment of 6 819. Average earnings of the enterprise heads in the sample were considerably higher than the SMIG, although 8 per cent of those in production and services and 16 per cent in clothing earned less than the SMIG. Of the wage-workers, 84 per cent earned more than the SMIG. The unskilled among them were the lowest paid. The majority of apprentices paid an apprenticeship fee but received meals and lodging; the apprenticeship fee amounted on average to one-third the value of the meals and lodging that the apprentices received from the entrepreneurs. The enterprise heads worked on average 53.5 hours per week; employees and apprentices worked on average about 50 hours per week. Average (mean) capital investment was $1 608 in production and services and $421 in clothing. The average value of capital assets per worker came to $365.

The customers of the informal sector were by and large themselves informals: 60 per cent of the turnover of the enterprises in the sample came from customers who were not wage-earners in the formal sector, 35 per cent were employees of the government, and 5 per cent consisted of sales to formal sector enterprises and state services. Linkages to the formal sector were stronger on the supply side: most production goods used by the informal sector came from the formal sector as did the bulk of raw materials and spare parts.

Nihan was struck by the relatively inefficient use of capital that appeared from the results of the Yaoundé informal sector survey - as had been the case of Nouakchott and Lomé: capital efficiency dropped with increases in equipment but the corresponding increases in labour productivity were smaller than would be expected. Nihan's explanation was that the informal sector entrepreneurs' investments (for which no depreciation provision was made) were only partly motivated by potential profitability; equipment also appeared as an embodiment of "wealth" and represented a form of saving protected from inflation and family demands on the entrepreneur.

f. Dakar (Senegal), 1988: A USAID-Funded Survey on the Nihan Model

A census of informal sector micro-entreprises of Dakar and its environs was carried out during the period September-October 1988 by USAID/Senegal for the Délégation à l'Insertion, la Réinsertion et l'Emploi of the Government of Senegal. A follow-up survey was carried out during the period November 1988-January 1989. The survey instrument used was a modified version of the questionnaire designed for Yaoundé by Georges Nihan.

The census of micro-enterprises in Dakar and its close environs (to Pikine and Thiaroye on the Cap Vert) identified almost 30 000 units employing some 57 000 persons including the enterpreneurs themselves. Almost three-quarters (72 per cent) of the units were in commerce; the other 28 per cent were in production, the building trades, services and transport. Average size of enterprise as measured by employment per unit ranged from 1.1 in trade to 8.1 in vehicle repair. The follow-up sample survey covered 558 micro-enterprises in production, building and services with no attempt made to include commerce and transport.

Of the micro-enterprises in the sample survey, 80 per cent had apprentices; that proportion reached 97 per cent for vehicle repair, 96 per cent for hairdressing and other services, and 87 per cent for woodworking. For the enterprises with apprentices, the average number of apprentices per enterprise was 4.7, ranging from 2.8 for the clothing sub-branch to 7.2 for vehicle repair. For those same enterprises, the apprentices made up 81 per cent of the work-force other than the enterprise head; in the case of vehicle repair, the proportion reached 87 per cent. The attraction of vehicle repair for apprentices reflects the fact that the activity is considered to be profitable and continually expanding.

The level of formal education of the apprentices was, as might be expected, quite low. Only 21 per cent had been to primary school (25 per cent for apprentices in the production sub-activities) and 3 per cent to middle school (5 per cent for the production sub-activities). None of the apprentices had attended a formal technical training institution.

For the sample as a whole, 30 per cent of the apprentices were family relations of the enterprise head; the other 70 per cent were recruited on a non-family basis. Almost 90 per cent of the enterprise heads included in the survey indicated that they received frequent requests to take on apprentices. The sub-activities most solicited were woodworking, metalworking, vehicle repair, electricity repair and hairdressing. The clothing sub-activity is less attractive than it used to be.

The survey questionnaire did not ask for any information concerning the sources of the inputs of the micro-enterprises of Dakar's informal sector. However, it was evident from casual observation that the sources of supply are varied. For many informal sector producers, the source of inputs is the formal sector retail shop across the street since most of the informal sector enterprises are too small to purchase at wholesale volumes. Often the source of supply is another informal sector producer working nearby. Another major source of inputs is recuperated waste products, most evident in the activities close to Dakar's formal sector industrial area which salvage and re-work cast-off remnants and discards of the factories. Metal workers obtain much of their raw material from the scrap metal merchants in Rebeusse. Car mechanics cannibalise spare parts from other automobiles brought in for repair or abandoned as scrap.

The questionnaire did ask for information on the customers of the micro-enterprises. Although 55 per cent of enterprises indicated that their main customers were households, the importance of other customers indicates that there are significant forward linkages to the formal sector as well as to other informal sector enterprises. Most (84 per cent) of the micro-enterprises work against specific orders; the other 16 per cent produce for inventory in the expectation of future sales. Only in metalworking and the building trades (in particular brick producers) does production for inventory reach as high as 33 per cent. The market relationships indicated in the 1988 survey are less restrictive than Chris Gerry's interpretation of them in his 1974 study discussed above.

Only 27 per cent of the entreprise heads who replied to the question concerning enterprise management procedures indicated that they kept an order book while 41 per cent replied that thay kept a receipts book; 19 per cent kept an account of receipts and expenditures, 29 per cent had a bank or savings account, but only 2.5 per cent kept a proper set of accounts while 4 per cent used or hired the services of someone to look after management problems. Very few had ever tried to get a bank loan.

The main tax to which the micro-enterprises are subject is the business license tax (*patente*), which is levied on individuals carrying out a commercial, industrial or professional activity. Only 24 per cent of the enterprise heads in the sample said that they paid the *patente*. Enterprises are also subject to a tax on business profits, a general income tax, a tax on services levied only on enterprises that have access to government contracts, and a stamp tax. Of the Dakar micro-enterprise sample, only 1 per cent paid anything on the business profits tax or the general income tax, 3 per cent paid the service tax, and 12 per cent paid the stamp tax.

The survey questionnaire contained an open question concerning the difficulties faced by the informal sector enterprise. Invariably lack of funds appeared at the top of the list, followed far behind by lack of customers and orders, and by difficulty in obtaining a business site. One quarter of the enterprise heads wanted mainly to keep the government out of their hair. The other three-quarters said that would like financial assistance from the government.

Lack of access to credit is the major felt need of the modern informal sector heads of enterprises. It is evident, however, that most of the micro-enterprises cannot provide the formal guaranties required by the formal banking system. Although there is a considerable volume of financial saving among the micro-enterprises themselves, a system of mutual saving and loan assocations has not yet developed.

4. Other Studies Commissioned out of ILO Headquarters

a. Khartoum (Sudan), 1976

A quick survey of the informal sector of the three towns of Khartoum (Khartoum, Khartoum North and Omdurman) was undertaken as part of the work of the 1976 ILO/UNDP employment strategy mission to Sudan[13]. Informal sector participants were identified through a sample survey of 2 614 households which included 5 300 participants (*i.e.* two per household) in informal sector activities excluding retail trade, distributed as follows: 42 per cent in manufacturing (food and beverages, leather footwear, wood products, repair of metal products), 17 per cent in repair services (electrical shops, motor vehicle and cycle repair), and 34 per cent in clothing. Of the informal sector enterprise heads, about 70 per cent had employees. One enterprise in ten operated from a variable location (one in three in motor vehicle repair). Forward linkages to the formal sector were insignificant: less than 1 per cent of the units sold to large enterprises, all of them in clothing.

b. Juba (Sudan), 1982-83

A study of the informal sector of Juba (Sudan) was undertaken by the ILO population and labour policies programme in 1982. According to William House[14], the formal sector in Juba consisted primarily of public sector administration and parastatal corporations along with a scattering of voluntary aid agencies, a few banking and insurance outlets, and churches and mosques; the informal sector consisted of small-scale manufacturing, construction, trade, transport, service and repair operations and a handful of self-employed professionals. It was estimated that in the mid-1980s, the informal sector involved 56 per cent of Juba's work-force and 61 per cent of all its household heads.

The ILO's Juba study was carried out in two phases: an initial mapping in late 1982 of all major concentrations of economic activity in Juba which located close to 2 500 enterprises; and a follow-up survey in early 1983 of a systematic random sample of 536 of those enterprises stratified by economic activity. The head of the enterprise was the sole owner in 80 per cent of the cases while the owner had at least one partner in 9 per cent; the other enterprises were headed by a manager, usually related to the owner. Only 9 per cent of the sample entrepreneurs were women, most of them in trade and a few in beer brewing: women engaged in home production for the market were not picked up in the original census unless they were actually outside the home as vendors. The mean number of workers per enterprise including the owner or manager was 2.5. One-man operations were widespread in petty trade, transport, and repairs; operations using more than one person were mostly in construction, auto repair and manufacturing but three-quarters of the enterprises employed at most one other worker in addition to the entrepreneur. Labour recruitment was done mostly through direct ethnic and kinship contacts. Child labour was prevalent although many of the young workers still attended school. Petty traders were mostly short-term Juba residents; proprietors in manufacturing, auto repairs and services were the longest-term residents of Juba which suggests that urban experience is necessary to acquire the skills required for those activities. Formal schooling of Juba's informal sector participants was low: 24 per cent of proprietors and 32 per cent of employees had never attended school, while an additional 45 per cent of proprietors and 41 per cent of employees had not gone beyond primary school.

Migrants to Juba made up 84 per cent of informal sector proprietors and 79 per cent of informal sector employees. Among proprietors, one-third of the migrants came from northern Sudan; northern Sudanese dominated the most capitalised and most profitable sectors of retail trade, transport and auto repair. Migrants to Juba from southern Sudan predominated among petty traders.

The activities where net income of Juba informal sector proprietors was highest were construction, restaurants and bars, retailing, transport, and auto repairs; the least profitable activities were tailoring, tinsmithing, petty trade, and repairs. Wage earnings were considerably lower than the average return to proprietors. Some 10 per cent of informal sector proprietors and 43 per cent of informal sector employees earned less than the minimum wage of a permanent government employee. The Juba survey showed that net business income of informal sector proprietors rose with years of education: income of the most educated was ten times that of those who had never been to school.

5. ILO/JASPA-PECTA Studies

The ILO's Jobs and Skills Programme for Africa - Programme des Emplois et des Compétences Techniques pour Afrique (JASPA-PECTA) carried out a number of informal sector surveys in the late 1970s and early 1980s in cities of both anglophone and francophone countries: Ougadougou (Burkina Faso), Banjul (The Gambia), Dar-es-Salaam (Tanzania), Brazzaville (Congo), Djibouti, Niamey (Niger), and Lusaka (Zambia). The results were summarised in a 1985 JASPA publication on the *Informal Sector in Africa*[15]. A more recent survey was fielded in Conakry and three provincial cities of Guinée[16].

a. Ouagadougou (Burkina Faso), 1977

The 1977 JASPA/PECTA informal sector survey of Ouagadougou organised by M.P. van Dijk covered 300 enterprises in manufacturing (42 per cent), artistic handicrafts (12 per cent), construction (9 per cent), retail trade (14 per cent), services (12 per cent), and transport (11 per cent). Small enterprises were identified as informal on the basis of three criteria: the enterprise had no juridical status (*i.e.* was unincorporated); enterprise personnel were not paid the legal minimum wage on a regular basis; and personnel were not enrolled with the Social Security Fund (*Caisse de sécurité sociale*). Women were concentrated mainly in batik-making and constituted 14 per cent of the sample. The average entrepreneur had been an apprentice for three years; only 8 per cent had obtained vocational training other than as an apprentice. Education levels were low: 46 per cent were illiterate; 13 per cent had attended coranic school; 9 per cent could read and write; 28 per cent had attended primary school; and 4 per cent had attended secondary school. A minority (31 per cent) of the entrepreneurs worked alone. The average size of enterprise for the sample as a whole was two persons (one of them an apprentice) per enterprise in addition to the entrepreneur. Most (88 per cent) of the entrepreneurs did not keep accounts. Average net earnings of the entrepreneurs came to 6 569 CFA francs ($26) per week; the average wage of the journeymen came to 2 990 CFA francs ($12) per week. Those apprentices who were paid (most were not) received on average 635 CFA francs ($2.50) per week.

b. Banjul (The Gambia), 1980

The 1980 ILO/JASPA survey of the informal sector of Banjul applied a questionnaire to 222 establishments in manufacturing and repair services with less than five paid employees in Kambo and St. Mary. Around half of the establishments were owned by non-Gambians. The 222 establishments employed 681 persons including the entrepreneurs themselves (34 per cent), partners (2 per cent), apprentices (54 per cent), paid employees (4 per cent), and unpaid family workers (6 per cent). Educational levels of the entrepreneurs were low: 80 per cent had never been to school. Most (86 per cent) of them had been trained as apprentices in the informal sector, 10 per cent as apprentices in the formal sector; 4 per cent had attended formal training institutions. Most of the apprentices working in the establishments in the sample were newly arrived migrants from rural areas. Apprentices received subsistence on a daily basis and some pocket money. Most of the apprentices paid a nominal fee for their training. The paid employees were paid on average 50 per cent above the legal minimum wage for the formal sector but without the fringe benefits provided by the formal sector. Since the Gambia's commercial economy is based on relatively unrestricted imports (mostly intended for re-export to its neighbours), most of the informal sector entrepreneurs complained about competition from imports, as well as about difficulties in obtaining working capital and suitable working premises.

c. Dar-es-Salaam (Tanzania), 1981

The 1981 JASPA survey of the informal sector of Dar-es-Salaam was carried out by the Economic Research Bureau of the University of Dar-es-Salaam in three wards in the suburbs and one in the city centre. The target establishments were production and repair activities employing less than ten persons. A questionnaire was applied to 71 establishments in woodworking, tailoring, leatherworking, metalworking and food processing. The average size of establishment was 4.5 persons. Wages received by paid employees were somewhat below the official minimum wage. Unpaid family labour accounted for 57 per cent of labour input; 17 per cent of the establishments had at least one apprentice. Apprentices were especially prevalent in woodworking.

d. Brazzaville (Congo), 1982

The 1982 PECTA survey of the informal sector of Brazzaville covered 77 enterprises with less than ten workers in commerce, handicrafts and services. The study destinguished between traditional handicrafts and modern handicrafts including woodworking. Services included electrical and mechanical repairs, transport, barbers, photographers, tailors, etc. For most of the enterprises, obtaining spare parts was their main problem.

e. Djibouti, 1982

The 1982 PECTA survey of the informal sector excluded the 85 per cent of the informal sector engaged in trade and transport. The survey covered 186 establishments and 250 entrepreneurs in production, construction, vehicle repair, artistic handicrafts, and other services. The average size of establishment was six persons including the owner; wage-earners constituted 59 per cent of the work-force, and apprentices 10 per cent (a remarkably low figure for Africa). Education levels were low: 44 per cent had not attended school; 39 per cent had attended coranic school; 14 per cent had some primary education; 3 per cent had some secondary education. The bulk (93 per cent) of the workers were males. The average wage of wage-earners was over twice the minimum wage in the formal sector; average monthly income was higher than the minimum wage for about two-thirds of the apprentices.

f. Niamey (Niger), 1982

The 1982 PECTA survey of the informal sector of Niamey covered 13 285 establishments in production, services, and commerce, 5 737 of them with fixed locations and 7 548 in itinerant activities. The average size of establishment was 1.6 persons. In fixed location activities, self-employed persons working alone accounted for 31 per cent of total labour input (52 per cent in commerce, 13 per cent in production). Wage-earners accounted for 26 per cent of the work-force in services, 15 per cent in production, and only 2 per cent in commerce. Apprentices constituted 29 per cent of the work-force in services and 35 per cent in production. Education levels were low: 76 per cent of owners and 70 per cent of wage-earners were illiterate or had attended only coranic school. The average wage of wage-earners was above the formal sector minimum wage in production and below the formal sector minimum wage in services.

g. Lusaka and Kitwe (Zambia), 1982

JASPA'S 1982 Zambia informal sector survey covered 711 enterprises in manufacturing, construction and repairs in Lusaka and Kitwe. The average size of enterprise was 2.2 persons including enterprise heads. The approximately 1 560 persons working in the sample enterprises included owners (48 per cent), partners (12 per cent), wage-workers (12 per cent), unpaid family workers (15 per cent) and apprentices (13 per cent). Only one in six enterprises employed more than two persons. On average, informal sector entrepreneurs had worked for six years in formal sector employment prior to setting up in business on their own. Two-thirds had some primary education; 20 per cent had received some formal training. Available infrastructure was weak: only 39 per cent had fixed work premises, 17 per cent had access to water, and 5 per cent had access to electricity (4 per cent had access to both electricity and water). Few of the entrepreneurs took on apprentices, preferring unpaid family workers. A relatively high number with formal sector jobs worked part-time in construction and in motor and radio repair.

h. Conakry, Kankan, Labé and Mamou (Guinée), 1987

The ILO JASPA/PECTA study of the informal sector of the four largest cities of Guinée[16] carried out a census of some 18 200 enterprises of which commerce accounted for 48 per cent, production for 19 per cent, services for 18 per cent, and transport for 15 per cent. Conakry, for which no transport activities were included, accounted for 53 per cent of the total for the four cities. Transport accounted for 48 per cent of the enterprises in Labé. The census was followed up by a sample survey.

In Conakry, 51 per cent of the enterprises had electricity but only 3 per cent had water. Equipment was limited: 66 per cent of the enterprises had only hand tools, 17 per cent had non-electric machine tools and 17 per cent had electric machine tools. The activities using relatively developed capital (in particular electric machine tools) were metal furniture making, vulcanisation, soldering, photography and automotive electricity. Activities using essentially manual technology were jewelry, brickmaking, metalworking, forges, fish smoking, carpeting and upholstery, painting, vehicle repair, and electrical repair. Enterprise equipment was financed primarily out of personal savings.

The average size of enterprise for the four cities was 4.1 workers including the enterprise head; in Conakry, it was 5.0. Close to half of the participants were apprentices (48 per cent for the four cities, 51 per cent in Conakry), 25 per cent were the enterprise heads (20 per cent in Conakry), 11 per cent were family workers (14 per cent in Conakry), and 7 per cent were partners of the enterprise head; only 9 per cent were wage-workers (8 per cent in Conakry).

Education levels were as follows (in per cent):

Level	Enterprise heads	Wage workers	Apprentices
No schooling	39	42	40
Coranic school only	22	16	11
Primary	20	25	36
Secondary	19	17	13
Total	100	100	100

The vast majority of the enterprise heads (86 per cent) had received their training on the job or as apprentices (79 per cent in Conakry); the proportion was even higher (93 per cent) for the wage-workers (89 per cent in Conakry).

The reported degree of compliance with regulations was high: 84 per cent of the enterprise heads said that they were registered and 75 per cent that they paid taxes.

Only 2 per cent of the enterprises kept proper accounts, 14 per cent kept a record of receipts and expenditures or an order book, while the other 84 per cent kept no accounts at all. Prices were determined by bargaining since only 34 per cent keep track of their costs.

Apprenticeship training was provided free; 58 per cent of the enterprises in Conakry guaranteed the subsistence of their apprentices. In Conakry 47 per cent of the wage-workers were former apprentices in the same enterprise; of the apprentices being trained at the time of the survey, 40 per cent were assured of being hired by the enterprise in which they were already working.

6. Other African Informal Sector Studies

a. Nairobi (Kenya), 1977

William House carried out a survey of Nairobi's informal sector in 1977 under the auspices of the Institute for Development Studies of the University of Nairobi[17]. The survey covered 577 heads of enterprises: 50 per cent in manufacturing, 21 per cent in trade, 28 per cent in services, and 1 per cent in land transport. Unlicensed taxis, female prostitutes, itinerant hawkers and petty traders were excluded. Manufacturing was over-represented in the sample.

Entry into the informal sector did not appear to be especially easy. Initial capital outlay was relatively low: over half the sample had invested less than KSL 500 ($67) to set up in business; however starting capital was much higher for the more remunerative activities such as furniture manufacturing, restaurants, and vehicle repair. The main problems were obtaining work space or premises, establishing a market, obtaining liquid capital, and harassment by the city police who were open to bribery. Between two-thirds and three-quarters of the enterpreneurs were in the 21-40 age group. Relatively recent migrants (those living in Nairobi for five years or less) accounted for 22 per cent of the enterpreneurs while only 2 per cent were born in Nairobi; 43 per cent of the entrepreneurs were landless. Employees in the informal sector were much younger and more recent migrants than their employers. For the employees the informal sector was a low-paid entry point into urban life.

Capital output and capital-to-labour ratios were much lower in the informal sector enterprises than in the formal sector in Kenya. Average net incomes accruing to informal sector enterpreneurs in Nairobi were considerably higher in trade than the mid-1977 legal minimum wage but lower in manufacturing (except for metalworking) and services (except for vehicle repair). Rural incomes overlapped in size with the lower range of incomes of informal sector households in the Nairobi sample. Among the factors significantly affecting income were the availability of capital and access to subcontracts. The branches receiving the most subcontracts were those with the highest incomes: furniture making, metalworking, and vehicle repair.

The number of workers per enterprise in the Nairobi sample including the enterprise head was 1.9. Of the employees, 54 per cent were employed on a regular basis, 12 per cent were intermittent or casual workers, and 34 per cent were apprentices. The 10 per cent of the employees who were unpaid included both family workers and apprentices.

b. Abidjan (Côte d'Ivoire), 1980-85: A sociologist's view

A humanist's view of the informal sector of Abidjan was presented in an entertaining book by Abdou Toure[18] describing the activities of a host of individuals doing odd jobs (les petits métiers) in the capital city of Côte d'Ivoire: pumping up car tyres that have been deflated by the police for illegal parking, "guarding" and washing cars, recuperating factory waste materials, itinerant tailoring, making soap, selling aphrodisiacs, washing muddy feet outside a market when it rains, providing the services of a public scribe, and many others. The number of individuals working on the street and in the market places is estimated to have more than doubled from 1976 to 1985, a rate of increase somewhat above that of the urban population of Abidjan. The petits métiers are carried out by both men and women.

Abidjan attracts migrants from all of the Sahel and the West African coast from Guinée to Nigeria. Each national group has different specialities. Ivorian males are car washers, auto mechanics, barbers, carpenters, building painters; Ivorian women are market sellers, hairdressers, prepared food sellers. Burkinabé (ex-Voltaïque) men are house guards, cooks, laundrymen, masons, itinerant vendors; Burkinabé women are cultivators and sellers of fresh vegetables. Malians are itinerant vendors, masons, metalworkers, auto mechanics, butchers, charcoal dealers; Malian women are soap-makers, coconut sellers, prepared food (brochettes) sellers, open-air hairdressers. Guinean men are auto mechanics, scrap metal workers, radio repairers, stall vendors, musicians; Guinean women are open-air hairdressers, prepared food sellers, cloth sellers, and popular singers. Ghanaian men are itinerant tailors, shoemakers, apothecaries, car washers; Ghanaian women (who outnumber male immigrants from Ghana) are food sellers and street prostitutes (the famous toutous, nomenclature derived from the pre-inflation price of a pass: two shilling tuppence). Men of the Niger are porters, itinerant vendors, coffee vendors, laundrymen, barbers and circumcisers, egg and fruit sellers, fish cleaners at the port, grilled meat sellers, shoemakers, itinerant fowl sellers; women of the Niger stay in Niger. Nigerian men are shopkeepers, market sellers, butchers, radio repairmen, auto mechanics, tyre repairers, informal money lenders, barbers; Nigerian women are itinerant vendors of beauty products, market sellers, itinerant hairdressers.

The invasion of the city by the street vendors and others has resulted in unsuccessful efforts by the Municipality to apply restrictions. More recently and more successfully, efforts are made to collect daily or monthly fees from street and market vendors. Repression is sporadic and ineffectual except as an incentive to pay off the police.

B. Asia

1. ILO urbanisation and employment research project studies [19]

a. Jakarta (Indonesia), 1975

The 1975 study of the informal sector of Jakarta by Hazel Moir and the Indonesian National Institute of Economic and Social Research (LEKNAS) sought to identify informal sector enterprises through individuals working in them, as identified by a household sample survey. The household survey covered 4 364 households. The sample households contained 5 359 informal sector participants, 4 367 of whom were enterprise heads. The majority of informal sector participants were men. The median age was 35 years for men and 39 years for women. Education levels were low: the median number of years of schooling for men and women combined was only three. Among men, 20 per cent had no schooling and 60 per cent had primary level or less; among women, 50 per cent had no schooling and 38 per cent had primary level or less. Migrants to Jakarta accounted for 60 per cent of the informal sector participants but recent migrants (those arriving within the five years prior to the survey) accounted for only 20 per cent. The main occupational categories were sales workers (63 per cent) and production workers (28 per cent). The proportion of sales workers was higher among migrants than among non-migrants.

The extent of occupational mobility was limited among Jakarta's informal sector participants as a whole, but there was a considerable amount of labour turnover among informal sector wage employees. More than 75 per cent of the participants stated that they did not want to change jobs at all.

Virtually all of the informal sector enterprises identified in the Jakarta sample were operated by sole proprietors, 90 per cent of whom worked alone. Most of the recently established enterprises were in commerce and services, which require relatively little capital. For the 10 per cent of enterprises employing workers in addition to the enterprise head, the average number of participants per enterprise (including the enterprise head) was 3.3. For the small number of enterprises for which wage information was forthcoming, wages paid in the informal sector were considerably lower than the minimum wages paid in the formal sector. The net earnings of the informal sector enterprise heads appeared to be well above the minimum wages prevailing in the formal sector.

The bulk (87 per cent) of the customers of the informal sector enterprises were households; forward linkages to the formal sector were virtually non-existent. Half of raw material purchases were made from small enterprises and 22 per cent relied on other sources; most of the others, particularly in trade, relied on households.

Compliance with regulations by Jakarta's informal sector was low except in transport: for the enterprises as a whole, only a quarter were registered and had a license; for transport the proportion was over half. Although about 40 per cent of the enterprise heads said they were recognised by the government, only a quarter claimed they were legal, 21 per cent said

41

they were inspected, and a small minority paid taxes. When asked what kinds of assistance they would like to receive, over three-quarters mentioned cheaper credit and over two-thirds wanted suitable business premises.

b. Manila (Philippines), 1976

The 1976 study by Gonzalo Jurado *et al.* of Manila's informal sector was carried out on the basis of an existing sampling frame of small enterprises with fewer than ten workers. The survey therefore probably overlooked very small enterprises without a fixed location. A sample of 3 500 was drawn, 71 per cent of which were in trade, 15 per cent in services and 12 per cent in manufacturing, with the small and under-represented remainder in construction and transport.

Of the 402 enterprises in manufacturing in the Manila sample, almost two-thirds were in textiles, wearing apparel and leather other than footwear, 11 per cent in food processing, 6 per cent in woodworking, 8 per cent in metalworking, and the rest in other branches. Because of the nature of the frame, most of the enterprises had a fixed location, operated in permanent structures, had access to water and electricity, were accessible through paved roads, were legally recognised, and were subject to government regulations or inspection. Average size of enterprise in terms of employment was 3.9 persons; however, almost half of the enterprise heads worked alone. Over 90 per cent of the workers were employed full-time. About a third of the participants were women. The average (mean) wage of hired workers was around the legal minimum wage, but a majority earned below that level; women received lower wages than men. The average wage in the sample enterprises was considerably lower than the average wage in the formal sector. Fixed assets (excluding land and buildings) came to around 8 000 pesos ($1 200) per enterprise or about 2 000 pesos ($300) per worker. However, the median value of fixed assets was only 3 000 pesos ($450). Recycling of capital goods appears to be of considerable importance since only 62 per cent of the enterprises purchased their equipment new while most of the remainder acquired their equipment second hand. Most of the customers were households. On the input side, 66 per cent of the enterprises relied on small enterprises and household enterprises for raw materials; 12 per cent relied on large commercial and government enterprises. The constraint most frequently cited (but by only 27 per cent of the enterprise heads) was lack of access to credit at moderate interest rates.

The Manila sample included enterprises in several forms of transport: jeepney buses, motorised tricycles, pedicabs (pedal-operated rickshaws), horse-drawn *caleshas*, and freight trucks. In many cases, the vehicles were leased on a daily basis. Average (mean) weekly earnings of the wage employees in informal sector transport were above the legal minimum wage but the median was below it. Net returns to the owners of the vehicles were quite high. The *caleshas* required relatively little capital and generated decent levels of income but they were on their way out because of competition from other forms of transport and because of public policies restricting their access to the central city because of traffic congestion and hygienic reasons.

Most of the enterprises in informal sector trade in the Manila sample were in fixed locations (because of the nature of the sampling frame). Half of them operated out of their residential premises. Almost all had the required government permit to operate. Over 60 per cent were open for business between 11 and 16 hours per day and most were open on Sundays and public holidays. The average size of enterprise was three persons, mostly family workers. Of the wage-workers, half were women. Wages were lower than in formal sector manufacturing. Most of the enterprise owners earned significantly more than the legal minimum wage even after making allowance for compensation of family workers.

Of the service enterprises in the Manila sample, more than half were located in the residences of the entrepreneurs. The average size of enterprise was 3.2 persons with 2.0 wage earners and 0.2 family workers per enterprise.

c. Colombo (Sri Lanka), 1977

The 1977 Marga Institute study of the informal sector of Colombo estimated the number of informal sector participants at 34 000 persons or 20 per cent of the labour force of the city. The authors attributed the relatively small size of the informal sector in Colombo to lack of growth of urban income in the Colombo region and the resulting lack of migration to Colombo.

The informal sector in Colombo was dominated by trade (63 per cent) including sales of prepared food; 20 per cent were in services, only 5 per cent in manufacturing, 8 per cent in transport, 1 per cent in construction, and 3 per cent in agriculture and fishing. Over 60 per cent of the enterprises in trade dealt in perishable commodities (vegetables, fruits, fish). In services, 43 per cent were self-employed unskilled casual labourers engaged in loading and unloading goods and 50 per cent were in repair services (automobiles, cycles, radios, locks). Those in manufacturing were engaged in tailoring, shoemaking and jewelrymaking. In transport, most were engaged in non-mechanised activities like pushcart and basket transport. Capital investment was low. The bulk (85 per cent) of the units were one-person enterprises; the average size of enterprise was 1.1 persons. Over 60 per cent of the units had been in operation over five years. Only a small number of women participated. There were fewer Sinhalese than Tamils and other ethnic groups among informal sector participants. Ethnicity and regional origin played a significant role: vegetable and fish vending were dominated by Sinhalese from the southern region of Sri Lanka; most of the individuals in non-mechanised transport activity were Tamils.

Earnings of the informal sector participants were low. However, most of the informal sector participants lived in multiple-person households containing additional earners from both the informal and formal sectors. Consequently their living conditions were relatively good: most lived in well-constructed houses with electricity, private water taps and toilet facilities.

The authors of the Colombo study saw the lack of dynamism of Colombo's informal sector as a reflection of the general stagnation of the city's economy. They drew the conclusion that attempts to provide direct assistance to informal sector enterprises would not lead to increased absorption of labour unless the process of economic development itself were accelerated.

2. ILO/ARTEP Informal Sector Surveys

a. Dhaka (Bangladesh), 1979

As reported by A.T.M. Nurul Amin a two-stage survey of informal sector activities in Dhaka was carried out in 1979[20]. An initial sample of 4 418 enterprises was selected in seven areas of the city where informal sector activity was known to be concentrated; 437

enterprises in the follow-up sub-sample were selected on the basis of a stratification of the initial sample by area, type of activity and size except for construction and transport which are not location-specific. Informality was defined by size (enterprises employing fewer than ten workers including the owner) and at least one of the following criteria: not registered under the Factory or Commercial Enterprise Establishment Acts; operating in an unauthorised location or otherwise illegally; located in a temporary structure or in a residence or backyard. The 437 enterprises in the sub-sample had 790 people working in them. Activities were grouped into five categories: trade (street selling and other petty retail trade); services (repair and other personal services); manufacturing (artisanal and other manufacturing activities); construction; and transport (rickshaws and other informal transport). The dominant retail activities were selling clothes (incuding imported second-hand clothes), food, betel, cigarettes, and (other) second-hand articles. Repairs accounted for two-thirds of services. Manufacturing included tailoring (31 per cent), metalworking (28 per cent), shoemaking and leatherworking (13 per cent), weaving (12 per cent) and furniture-making (11 per cent). Construction work included unskilled activities (78 per cent) such as earth-digging, working as assistants to masons, and brick-breaking to produce aggregate for making concrete, and skilled activities (22 per cent) such as carpentry, painting, masonry and plumbing. Rickshaws made up half the informal transport sample, the other half being three-wheel vehicles, push carts and bullock carts. Self-employed and enterprise heads accounted for 45 per cent of the labour force, hired labour (including independent construction workers hired on a daily basis and transport workers who do not own their own vehicles) for 36 per cent and family labour for 20 per cent. Female participation in informal sector activity is low in Dhaka except in construction where women account for 20 per cent of the labour force. The informal sector labour force is relatively young with 47 per cent under 25 years of age. Education levels are lower than in the formal sector: 31 per cent of the informal sector sample had never been to school in contrast to 2 per cent of a small sample drawn from the formal sector; 17 per cent of the informals had some secondary schooling in contrast to 87 per cent for the formals; and only one per cent of the informals had completed secondary school as compared with 50 per cent of the formals. Recent migrants (with under five years of residence in Dhaka) made up 44 per cent of the informals. Most owners of informal sector enterprises had been living in Dhaka much longer than their employees. Earnings in the informal sector, particularly among the self-employed, were higher than those of wage earners in the formal sector and some 15 per cent higher than the average rural household. Capital intensity (capital to labour ratio) in informal sector manufacturing was only 13 per cent of that in formal sector manufacturing; the relation for labour productivity was 46 per cent.

The Dhaka informal sector survey provided many examples of innovation and adaptability in recycling of scrap metals, engines and vehicle tyres and in production and repair of household items mostly using second-hand materials.

Nurul Amin's article points up a common anomaly faced by informal sector participants: the existence of licence requirements which are not enforced but which provide a pretext for harassment and extortion by the police.

b. Bangkok (Thailand), 1986

The 1986 ILO/ARTEP sample survey of self-employed and small proprietors in Bangkok[21] identified 235 such individuals in two districts of Bangkok (central Bangkok and a recently settled suburb called Huay Kwang) through a four-stage sampling procedure involving a) selection of the two districts, b) selection of 30 sampling blocks each containing about 100 households, c) a complete census of the 3 990 households in the 30 sampling blocks, and d) a systematic sub-sample by activity of 235 out of the 1 077 self-employed and small proprietors in the 3 990 households. Activities identified included enterprises with a single owner or jointly owned with a partner. An upper limit of ten hired workers was imposed with no limit for family workers. Self-employed professionals and money lenders were excluded. Of the 1 077 self-employed, 45 per cent were in trade, 8 per cent in manufacturing, and 27 per cent in services; 51 per cent were males, 49 per cent females. The average number of workers including the enterprise head was 3.5, varying from 1.7 for cleaning services to 9.0 for the other manufacturing category. The weighting of the sub-sample of 235 was purposely biased to come up with 33 per cent in trade, 35 per cent in manufacturing, and 32 per cent in services. The average number of workers including the enterprise head was 3.2, of which 0.8 unpaid family workers per enterprise. The smallest enterprises were in street and stall vending and transport; the largest were in metalworking and jewelry making. The majority (82 per cent) operated from permanent structures, usually the house of the entrepreneur.

Women constituted 45 per cent of the sub-sample: 60 per cent of the self-employed and enterprise heads in trade, 39 per cent in manufacturing, and 36 per cent in services. Among the paid employees, women predominated in garment manufacture, beauty salons and hairdressing; they were a majority in leatherworking.

The entrepreneurs were all 30 years of age or older; 66 per cent were over 50. The hired and family workers were mostly (79 per cent) below 30 years of age; 2 per cent were under 14. Education levels were somewhat higher among the workers than among the entrepreneurs: 69 per cent of the workers had completed primary education, 60 per cent of the entrepreneurs. Among the self-employed and enterprise heads, the level of education was below the average in trade and above the average in services, with manufacturing in between. Among the workers, 12 per cent were paid a daily wage, 39 per cent were salaried, 18 per cent worked on piece-rate contracts, and 31 per cent were unpaid.

Most of the entrepreneurs were long-time residents of Bangkok: over two-thirds had lived there for twenty years or more. Recent migrants were much more frequent among the paid and family workers.

Forward linkages to the formal sector were appreciable: 20 per cent had received sub-contracts from larger firms, particularly in garment making and jewelry making. The main problems created by subcontracting were fluctuations in the level of orders and delays in payments by the firms issuing the subcontracts.

The self-employed and enterprise heads in the sample generally earned considerably more than the average urban wage-worker.

The source of funds to start their business for most (82 per cent) of the entrepreneurs was their own savings (which explains the relatively advanced ages of the entrepreneurs in the sample); 15 per cent obtained loans from family or friends, 1 per cent from a financial institution, and 2 per cent from other sources. The most commonly cited difficulty experienced in setting up in business was obtaining credit. Most of the entrepreneurs had received their training on the job, 43 per cent in a previous work place and 20 per cent in a family business; 18 per cent had received at least some formal vocational training or higher education, 2 per cent learned from other sources, and 17 per cent had no training at all before starting their business.

3. Other Asian Informal Sector Surveys

a. Four Indian Provincial Cities: Wardha, Ghaziabad, Allahabad and Jaipur, 1986

A survey of 2 000 informal sector enterprises in four provincial cities of India was carried out in 1986 by the National Institute of Urban Affairs of New Delhi for the Ministry of Urban Development of the Government of India: 200 in Wardha (Maharashtra), 400 in Ghaziabad (Uttar Pradesh), 600 in Allahabad (Uttar Pradesh), and 800 in Jaipur (Rajasthan)[22]. Wardha is a small service-oriented city with a population of around 100 000. Ghaziabad is an industrial city close to Delhi with a population of around 300 000. Allahabad is an administrative and industrial city of around 700 000. Jaipur, the capital of Rajasthan, has a population of around 1.0 million; its economy has a sizeable industrial component.

The definition used to identify informal sector activity was any enterprise employing less than ten persons and not coming under the purview of the Shops and Establishments Act.

The sectoral distribution by city of the 2 000 informal sector entrepreneurs in the sample was as follows (in per cent):

City	Manufacturing	Services & repairs	Commerce	Construction	Transport	Total
Wardha	21	31	32	5	11	100
Ghaziabad	7	44	26	12	11	100
Allahabad	18	38	37	2	5	100
Jaipur	25	13	36	4	22	100

For the four cities combined, 70 per cent of the enterprises in the sample were single-person enterprises, 28 per cent employed between two and five persons, and only 2 per cent employed between six and nine persons. Over half operated in a physical structure: 35 per cent in durable (*pucca* or *semi-pucca*) structures and 19 per cent in non-durable (*kutcha*) structures; the rest worked in the open: 17 per cent in fixed locations and 29 per cent itinerant. Most of the enterprises worked with relatively little capital: the average amount of capital investment per enterprise was 8 190 rupees ($650). Average turnover per enterprise was 41 650 rupees ($3.303); average net income per enterprise was 9 230 rupees ($732). The averages by branch of activity were as follows (in rupees):

Branch of activity	Capital per enterprise per enterprise	Annual sales turnover per enterprise	Annual net income
Manufacturing	9 700	49 965	10 262
Commerce	8 620	5 188	39 349
Service & repairs	6 860	31 857	9 406
Construction	5 740	57 291	7 489
Transport	10 220	19 215	7 770
All branches	8 190	41 650	9 230

Forward linkages from informal sector producers to the formal sector were weak: 94 per cent of sales were made to households, 4 per cent to local shops and hawkers, and 2 per cent to formal sector manufacturing units. With respect to backward linkages, 87 per cent of the informal sector enterprises bought their raw materials locally (41 per cent from registered wholesalers and 46 per cent from retailers and hawkers), 12 per cent from formal sector manufacturers, and 1 per cent from households.

b. Delhi and Five Other Cities in India's National Capital Region, 1987

A 1987 survey of the informal sector in Delhi and five other cities in India's National Capital Region was carried out in three stages[23]. The first stage applied a light questionnaire to 1 180 informal sector enterprises in the National Capital Region: 270 in Tri Nagar and 220 in Vishwas Nagar (two sections of the Union Territory of Delhi), 98 in Sonepat and 149 in Faridabad (both in Haryana), 100 in Ghaziabad and 200 in Khurja (both in Uttar Pradesh), and 143 in Alwar (Rajasthan). The second stage applied a more detailed questionnaire to a sub-sample of 143 of those enterprises. The third stage applied a supplementary labour force oriented questionnaire to a sample of 485 households living in the localities where the informal sector activities were concentrated.

Registration of the 1 180 informal sector units with the Small Scale Industries Department of their respective States or with a local body was fairly extensive but variable: 50 per cent on average, 90 per cent in Alwar, 87 per cent in Khurja, 71 per cent in Ghaziabad, 62 per cent in Sonepat, 43 per cent in Vishwas Nagar, 28 per cent in Faridabad and 8 per cent in Tri Nagar. However, most had fewer than five workers, did not adhere to labour laws, and had large family participation. The breakdown by branch of activity was 81 per cent in manufacturing, 13 per cent in assembling, 4 per cent in wholesale trade, and 2 per cent in retail trade. There was some degree of specialisation in the different geographical clusters: Khurja in manufacture of pottery and ceramics, Tri Nagar in plastic and PVC products, Vishwas Nagar in cables, utensils and PCV products, and Alwar, Faridabad, Ghaziabad and Sonepat in light engineering and metal goods. The typical informal sector entrepreneur in the National Capital Region was in the middle age group (21-40), resident in the town of birth, or from another part of the region, speaking the local language as mother tongue, with moderate education and no formal training in his sphere of activity. They had picked up their expertise on the job, 22 per cent of them as apprentices.

The average number of persons employed per enterprise in the larger sample was 7.5 including the enterprise head: 13 per cent entrepreneurs, 65 per cent regular employees, 17 per cent casual workers, and 5 per cent family workers. In the opinion of the authors of the survey report, employment as reported by the respondents underestimated employment by 25 to 30 per cent, including unreported female family workers. Average employment per enterprise in the sub-sample was 7.3, close to the 7.5 of the initial sample, but the proportion of regular employees was only 56 per cent and that of casual employees 30 per cent. Skilled workers constituted 57 per cent of the regular employees in the sub-sample and 33 per cent of the casual workers. The hierarchy of average wage ratios by category was as follows: unskilled casual, 1.0; unskilled regular, 1.5; skilled casual, 1.6; and skilled regular, 2.3. Average capital investment per enterprise in the larger sample was 67 000 rupees ($5.170), but the median was much lower. Of the financing of capital investment, 84 per cent came from personal saving or from the immediate family, friends or relatives, 15 per cent from cumulated profits, and 1 per cent from banks and other sources. The ratio of annual sales turnover to capital was 1.9. The estimated rate of return on investment (profit divided by investment) was 17.8 per cent; the rate of return on sales (profit divided by sales) was 4.2 per cent.

The informal sector enterprises in the Indian National Capital Region sample had negligible forward linkages to the formal sector. Backward linkages (purchases from formal sector units) were a little stronger. Linkages were strong among informal sector enterprises, mostly within 5 kms of each other.

C. Latin America

This section reviews a sample of the studies of the informal sector in Latin America that have been carried out since the mid-1970s under the auspices of the ILO in Geneva, ILO/PREALC in Santiago, and other institutions.

1. ILO Urbanisation and Employment Research Project Studies

The ILO urbanisation and employment research project commissioned studies of the urban informal sector in three cities of Latin America: Bogota (Colombia), Campinas (Brazil) and Cordoba (Argentina)[24].

a. Bogota (Colombia), 1974

The 1974 study on the informal sector of Bogota, carried out by OFISEL Ltda. under the direction of Oscar Marulanda Gomez in collaboration with Cecilia de Castillo, was an attempt to describe the characteristics of informal sector activities and the labour force participating in those activities as identified through a household survey rather than through an establishment or enterprise survey. The procedure followed was to take a sample of households in Bogota and to administer to each working member of each household a survey instrument containing questions, *inter alia*, on the characteristics of the establishments where they worked. The intended size of the sample was 800 households (out of the 510 000 households in Bogota at the time). The size of the sample actually included in the survey was 562 households with 2 989 members, of whom 831 were working members;

777 of the working members were interviewed. The sample households were selected on a random basis from the 63 *barrios* of the city stratified by income on the basis of information obtained from earlier surveys.

Establishments were classified into four categories: a) individual units with no fixed place of work (mostly in commerce and personal services); b) family units (small enterprises employing predominantly family workers); c) small- and medium-scale enterprises (SMEs) using some wage-workers; and d) large-scale enterprises with more than ten workers. Of the four, the first two were (except for a few professionals) clearly in the informal sector. The SME category was largely formal but with informal components. The distribution of the working population by category of establishment as estimated from the survey was the following (in per cent): self-employed invididual units, 15; family units, 28; SMEs, 32; large-scale enterprises, 25. In other words, at least 43 per cent of the working population of Bogota worked in the informal sector. Of those working in the two categories of establishments making up the bulk of the informal sector (self-employed individuals and family units), 36 per cent were in commerce and 22 per cent were in personal services.

A number of other characteristics that define the frontier between formality and informality were also examined. For example, the differing proportions of the production units in Bogota showing certain characteristics of informality in each of the four categories of establishments were as follows (in per cent):

Characteristics of informality	Self-employed	Family units	SMEs	Large-scale enterprises	Average
1. Non-compliance with legal norms	74	38	11	2	16
2. Non-application of work accident prevention measures	72	46	34	13	32
3. Non-affiliation to social security system	100	76	34	26	52
4. Informal training	88	68	44	28	50

b. Campinas (Brazil), 1976

The informal sector in Campinas was defined in the 1976 study by Manuel Tosta Berlinck to consist of a) own-account workers (working with or without unpaid family labour) and b) small enterprises with fewer than ten wage-workers. The survey covered a sample of 500 units, 20 per cent of which were in industry, 40 per cent in commerce and 40 per cent in services; 90 per cent were legally registered with the appropriate authorities. The distribution by capital size was 26 per cent with capital of less than 10 000 cruzeiros ($930), 31 per cent with capital between 10 000 and 50 000 cruzeiros ($4 650), and 43 per

49

cent with capital above 50 000 cruzeiros. In 81 per cent of the cases, purchase of machinery and equipment was financed through own savings; in only 8 per cent was the purchase of equipment financed by bank loans.

Most (88 per cent) of the Campinas informal sector enterprise heads were males. The distribution of enterprise heads by education level was as follows: 2 per cent illiterate, 15 per cent with incomplete primary education, 41 per cent with complete primary education and 42 per cent with more than primary education. Although 78 per cent of the enterprise heads were immigrants to Campinas (73 per cent from other parts of Brazil and 5 per cent from abroad) only one-third of the immigrants had been in Campinas less than ten years; most (73 per cent) of the immigrants came from other urban areas. About three-quarters of the informal sector enterprise heads had earlier worked as wage-earners in the formal sector. Over half of the enterprise heads acquired the savings to finance their initial capital out of wage income.

Of the 500 sample units, 46 per cent were one-person enterprises, 17 per cent had family workers but no wage workers, and 37 per cent employed wage workers (as well as some family workers). Average employment was 2.74 persons per enterprise, including the enterprise heads.

Backward linkages to the formal sector (purchase of inputs) were strong. Forward linkages were weak: only 12 per cent of sales were made to enterprises. Most (90 per cent) of sales were made locally to customers in Campinas.

c. Cordoba (Argentina), 1976

The 1976 study of Cordoba, the centre of the automotive and engineering industry in Argentina, by Carlos E. Sanchez *et al.* focused on enterprises employing five persons or less in addition to the enterprise head. The study distinguished between relatively high income activities (called quasi-formal) and relatively low income activities (called informal). A considerable number of "quasi-formal" enterprises with less than five workers earned relatively high incomes because of advanced skills, high capital intensity, or oliogopolistic market conditions in activities that included self-employed professionals (doctors, lawyers, etc.), small engineering and other manufacturing units with a significant endowment of skills and investments, self-employed construction workers including plumbers and electricians, and capital-intensive commerce. The informal sector included low-income activities such as unskilled self-employed construction workers, domestic servants (mostly women), porters, gardeners, etc.

The Cordoba survey results were based on a sample of almost 2 500 enterprise heads drawn from two sampling frames, one based on enterprises with fixed locations and the other based on households (to identify self-employed workers without a fixed location). The number of persons participating in the quasi-formal and informal sectors of Cordoba's economy came to 38 per cent of the town's active population (23 per cent quasi-formal and 15 per cent informal). Since domestic servants were defined as part of the informal sector, the proportion of women among informal sector participants was high (63 per cent) compared to only 23 per cent in the quasi-formal sector. The level of education of both quasi-formal and informal sector participants was lower than for the economically active population as a whole: 56 per cent of Cordoba's active population had eight or more years of education; the proportion was 39 per cent for quasi-formal sector participants and 18 per cent for informal sector participants. Of the two groups combined, 30 per cent were in trade (including restaurants) and 38 per cent were in services (including domestic service).

Income levels in the informal sector of Cordoba were low by virtue of the definition used. However, some 24 per cent of quasi-formal own-account workers without a fixed location were also in the lowest income group (below 80 000 pesos or $71 per month). Only 24 per cent of the quasi-formal enterprise heads received more than 400 000 pesos or $357 per month. Only one-third of the enterprise heads in the two groups combined made more than the 1973 national average income of 154 000 pesos ($137) per month.

2. ILO/PREALC Informal Sector Studies

a. Latin America and the Caribbean: the PREALC Approach

PREALC has taken a labour market approach to the informal sector. Initially, the PREALC view was that informality was primarily a result of an excess availability of labour for employment in the formal sector and that informal sector activity was entered into only as an alternative to open unemployment. The results of household surveys in several countries were used to estimate the share of the informal sector activities in labour force participation. Informal sector activities were defined to include: domestic servants; casual workers; own-account workers; and all persons (employers, employees, hired workers and family workers) working in enterprises employing four persons or fewer. Alternatively, identifying informality with low productivity and low income, individuals with income below a certain minimum (usually the legal minimum wage) were defined as informal[25]. The expectation was that informal sector activities would ultimately be replaced or absorbed by an expanding formal sector and that the informal sector participants would end up as wage earners in the formal sector.

	Per cent
Manufacturing	19
Construction	6
Commerce	20
Fixed location	(16)
Itinerant	(4)
Transport	3
Services	38
Other	14
Total	100

PREALC's estimates of the share of the informal sector in the urban labour force in eleven selected Latin American countries in the late 1960s or early 1970s are reproduced in Table 2.1 according to one or the other of the two criteria cited above (occupation or income). The shares ranged from 30 per cent in Brazil to 57 per cent in Paraguay, with an average figure of around 34 per cent for the countries specified in the table.

The PREALC estimates of the distribution of the urban informal sector labour force by branch of activity in Latin America around 1970 are shown in Table 2.2. The largest group was services (including domestic servants), followed by commerce and then by manufacturing as indicated below.

Services predominated (40 per cent or over) in Brazil, Chile, Ecuador, El Salvador and Paraguay. Manufacturing accounted for over 20 per cent of informal sector activity in Chile, Colombia, Ecuador and Mexico. Commerce was dominant in Argentina (41 per cent).

Table 2.1

INFORMAL SECTOR SHARE OF THE URBAN LABOUR FORCE
IN SELECTED COUNTRIES OF LATIN AMERICA
(Per cent)

Country and city	Occupational basis[1]	Income basis[1]	Revised estimates ("around 1970")[2]
Argentina			
Cordoba	-	-	37.6
Brazil			
States of Rio de Janeiro & Sao Paulo (1972)	-	24	-
Total urban	-	-	30.3
Chile			
Total urban (1968)	39	-	39.9
Colombia			
Bogota	-	-	43.4
Dominican Republic			
Santo Domingo (1973)	-	50	55.0
Ecuador			
Guayaquil (1970)	-	48	-
Other (1970)	-	48	-
Total urban	-	-	45.4
El Salvador			
San Salvador (1974)	46	41	46.0
Mexico			
Federal District & Mexico State (1970)	-	27	-
Federal District, Guadalajara & Monterrey	-	-	41.5
Paraguay			
Asuncion (1973)	57	-	57.0
Peru			
Total urban (1970)	60	-	33.1
Venezuela			
Total urban (1970)	44	-	44.0
Caracas (1970)	40	-	-
Total	-	-	34.4

Source : 1. Paulo R. Souza and Victor E. Tokman, "The Urban Informal Sector in Latin America", in *International Labour Review*, Vol. 114, No. 3, November-December 1976, Table 1, p. 398.

2. Victor E. Tokman, "Politicas para el sector informal en America Latina", in *Revista internacional del trabajo*, Vol. 97, No. 3, July-September 1978, p. 314.

Table 2.2

URBAN INFORMAL SECTOR BY BRANCH OF ACTIVITY
IN SELECTED COUNTRIES OF LATIN AMERICA AROUND 1970
(Per cent)

Country	Manufacturing	Construction	Commerce		Transport	Services	Other	Total
			Fixed location	Itinerant				
Argentina	14.1	9.5	40.7[1]	n.c.	3.2	30.2	2.3	100.0
Brazil	18.0	8.2	11.3	4.8	3.4	42.3	12.0	100.0
Chile	22.8	6.6	26.1[1]	n.c.	4.1	40.4	-	100.0
Colombia	29.5	-	36.2[1]	n.c.	6.2	25.0	3.1	100.0
Dominican Republic	19.0	8.0	23.0	15.0	-	33.0	2.0	100.0
Ecuador	21.8	3.1	25.2[1]	n.c.	3.9	42.0	4.0	100.0
El Salvador	12.0	4.0	17.0	14.0	-	49.0	4.0	100.0
Mexico	22.7	6.4	12.3	3.5	2.2	39.3	13.6	100.0
Paraguay	18.0	6.0	20.0	8.0	-	40.0	8.0	100.0
Peru	17.2	5.4	19.0	7.6	6.0	26.8	18.0	100.0
Venezuela	13.0	-	28.0[1]	n.c.	-	23.0	36.0	100.0
Total	18.6	6.3	16.4	4.0	3.3	37.5	13.9	100.0

Note : 1. Included with fixed location commerce.

Source: Victor E. Tokman, "Politicas para el sector informal en America Latina", *op. cit.*, p. 314, see Table 2.1 above.

The PREALC discussions distinguished from the beginning between branches of activity in which informal sector enterprises can hold their own in a market dominated by the formal sector (personal services, repair services, small-scale fixed-location retail trade, artistic handicrafts, tailors and dressmakers) and marginal activities destined to disappear over the long run as the overall economy expands (itinerant vending of non-food articles, domestic service, shoe-shining, guarding automobiles)[26]. In some sub-branches of manufacturing, technologies suitable to small-scale production and competitive with those used in larger scale formal sector production are available or already in use.

In his look at "The Informal Sector: 15 Years Later"[27], Victor Tokman found that the informal sector did not shrink significantly during the period of growth of the 1970s while it has probably expanded in the situation of economic crisis of the 1980s. The rise in open unemployment resulting from the contraction of economic activity in the 1980s led to an increase in public sector employment in Chile while informal sector employment rose rapidly in Brazil and Peru. The continued existence of informal sector activities is determined by two basic economic conditions: labour surplus and limited access to markets and to productive resources.

The heterogeneity of the informal sector has become more apparent in the light of new empirical studies focused on informal sector establishments as economic units rather than on the labour force employed in them. Little or no capital is required for domestic service or street vending, whereas more capital is required to set up as a taxi driver or a small shopkeeper. Income differentials are considerable between domestic servants and workers in informal sector enterprises, and between such workers, the self-employed and informal sector enterprise owners. The range of incomes is, nevertheless, narrow. The PREALC view is that the informal sector can develop only in gaps in the market left open by the formal sector, and that incomes tend to be kept low since entry into the informal sector is generally unrestricted and relatively easy because of low capital requirements.

Mobility out of the informal sector into the formal sector appears to be low, probably because of the low levels of education of informal sector workers and possibly because of a lack of transferability of skills. Female domestic servants leave the labour market when they marry and start to raise their own families. To the extent that the time of family labour is shared between work in the informal sector enterprise and household work or other uses, family labour is relatively immobile.

PREALC's 1978 review of *El Sector Informal: Funcionamiento y Politicas*[28] presented, *inter alia*, the results of several general studies of the informal sector in a number of cities including Asuncion (Paraguay), Mexico City, Guadalajara, and Monterrey (Mexico), San Salvador (El Salvador), Quito and Guayaquil (Ecuador), and Kingston (Jamaica) as well as detailed studies of specific informal activities in San Salvador, Santiago (Chile) and Kingston. A more recent PREALC book has examined street vending in Santiago[29].

b. Mexico City, Guadalajara and Monterrey (Mexico), 1970

The size of the urban informal sector in three major cities of Mexico (Mexico City, Guadalajara and Monterrey) was estimated from the 1970 population census on two alternative criteria: a) all non-agricultural labour force participants with monthly incomes less than 699 pesos (high estimate), and b) non-salaried workers with monthly incomes less than 699 pesos in all occupations except the unspecified category plus domestic servants who are all considered to be informal (low estimate). For all of Mexico, the high estimate yielded a figure of 3.2 million and the low estimate 2.2 million. For the three cities, the high estimate was 1.2 million and the low estimate 0.8 million.

The breakdown of the high estimate of the urban informal sector labour force by branch at the national level was estimated at 32 per cent in industrial activities (manufacturing, mining, construction, energy), 16 per cent in commerce, 36 per cent in services (including domestic service) and transport, and 16 per cent unspecified.

For the three cities, the informal sector occupied between 75 and 76 per cent of the urban labour force, between 51 and 62 per cent of the women in the labour force (if domestic services are included in the informal sector), between 48 and 56 per cent of the labour force under 25 years of age, between 14 and 19 per cent of the labour force over 50 years of age, and between 43 and 59 per cent of those in the labour force with less than four years of primary education.

c. Asuncion (Paraguay), 1973

On the basis of a household survey of Greater Asuncion carried out in 1973, 57 per cent of the labour force was in the informal sector (defined to include own-account workers, workers in enterprises employing less than five persons, casual workers, and domestic servants). Participation in the informal sector was higher for women (because of the inclusion of domestic servants) than for men. The youngest and oldest workers were concentrated in the informal sector, as were migrants: 82 per cent of recent migrants (in Asuncion for less than one year) and 71 per cent for longer-term migrants (those who arrived in Asuncion in the ten years preceding the date of the survey). Informal sector participants of both sexes had lower educational qualifications and lower incomes than workers in the formal sector. The number of workers in the informal sector was greater than those in the formal sector in all branches of activity except banking and finance, basic services, and government. The ratio of average incomes in the formal sector to those in the informal sector was 2.6 on average: 2.8 for manufacturing, 1.5 for fixed-location commerce, 2.7 for itinerant commerce, 1.5 for repairs and maintenance, and 2.9 for other private services. The average income in the Asuncion informal sector of individuals with less than three years of education was only 1.6 times the average income in traditional small farming in Paraguay, a ratio that may explain the relatively low rate of migration from rural Paraguay into Asuncion during the period 1962 to 1972.

d. San Salvador (El Salvador), 1974

The PREALC evaluation of the size and characteristics of the informal sector in San Salvador was derived from a 1974 household labour force survey. Informal sector participants were taken to include own account workers with less than thirteen years of education (to exclude the liberal professions), casual workers, all those working in enterprises with less than four persons (owners, employees, casual workers, and family workers), and domestic servants. On that basis, 46 per cent of the labour force worked in the informal sector. The breakdown by sex was 29 per cent for men and 63 per cent for women when domestic servants were included as informal; it was 28 per cent for men and 31 per cent for women if domestic servants were excluded from the definition. Education levels were much lower in the informal sector than in the formal sector: 73 per cent of those in the labour force with only 0-3 years of education were in the informal sector. Newly arrived migrants were predominantly informal sector participants since 55 per cent of migrants arriving in San Salvador during the year prior to the survey were domestic servants. The breakdown by branch of activity of informal sector participants was 12 per cent in manufacturing, 5 per cent in construction, 39 per cent in commerce, 28 per cent in services and other activities, and 16 per cent in domestic service. Average income in the informal sector was only 38 per cent of average income in the formal sector. For the working population with 0-6 years of education, incomes were lower in the informal sector than in the formal sector; for those with more than six years of education, incomes in the informal sector were higher than in the formal sector. For wage and salary workers alone, however, incomes were consistently lower in the informal sector.

PREALC also analysed the results of a census of small-scale commerce in San Salvador covering street vendors (established and itinerant) and vendors in the markets on the perimeter of the city. Of the vendors, 90 per cent were women. Itinerant street vendors were younger and less educated than the established vendors since itinerant vending is a labour market entry activity.

e. Quito and Guayaquil (Ecuador), 1968 and 1973

A PREALC analysis of the informal sector in Ecuador was based on the results of a 1968 nationwide urban household survey and two surveys of poor urban households in 1973 and 1974. The informals, defined as those in the working population receiving less than the prevailing minimum wage, constituted 52 per cent of Ecuador's urban labour force; 35 per cent of the urban informals were in Quito and Guayaquil, 61 per cent were males, 45 per cent were under 25 years of age, and 41 per cent were either illiterate or had less than three years of schooling. Their distribution by branch of activity was 33 per cent in personal services (including domestic servants), 26 per cent in manufacturing, 21 per cent in commerce, 10 per cent in agriculture and livestock, 5 per cent in transport and communications, and 5 per cent in building and other activities. In Guayaquil and Mochala Puerto Bolivar, the majority of informals were migrants since entry into informal sector activities is relatively easy. The study postulates the movement of low-income landless rural workers into the urban informal sector where per capita income is somewhat higher.

f. Kingston (Jamaica), 1974

An estimate of the size of the informal sector in Jamaica was derived from the results of a 1974 labour force survey by applying some bold assumptions to the numbers of owners and wage-workers in establishments with less than ten workers, own-account workers, unpaid family workers, and domestic servants. Since three-quarers of Jamaica's urban population was concentrated in Kingston, it was estimated that one-third of the urban labour force lived on incomes generated in the informal sector.

g. Santiago (Chile), 1976 and 1988

A survey of small food shops carried out in 1973 by PREALC and Chile's SENDE (Servicio Nacional del Emploi) provided data for analysing competition between informal sector food sellers and supermarkets in Santiago. The market power of the supermarkets results in lower raw material costs, greater economies of scale, and lower prices than those of their informal sector competitors. Nevertheless, the small food shops have survived and flourished by dint of their physical and temporal proximity to their customers: the small food shops are located off the main thoroughfares and in the side streets of the poorer neighbourhoods of Santiago, and they stay open longer hours and sell in smaller units than the supermarkets. The average net income of owners of small food shops was about 1.9 times the official minimum wage if imputed payments to working family members are deducted from receipts.

The 1988 PREALC study of illegal itinerant street vendors of Santiago turned up some interesting facts: 65 per cent of the street vendors were male, 35 per cent female; 75 per cent were between 20 and 44 years of age; education levels were relatively high with 40 per cent having some secondary level education and another 14 per cent having completed secondary school. The study also threw light on some of the competitive and complementary relationships between the formal sector shops and the informal street vendors. On the complementary side, some of the formal sector retail shops derived part of their business from supplying goods to the street vendors for resale to customers to whom they would not otherwise have access, while some of the formal sector shops also provided safe haven for the street vendors during police raids.

3. Other Latin American Informal Sector Studies

a. Belo Horizonte (Brazil), 1972

Thomas Merrick's review of a 1972 household survey focused on labour force characteristics of 2 445 households, carried out as part of the metropolitan area plan for Belo Horizonte[30], defined the informal sector's labour force to include all workers who did not contribute to a social security institute (other than the liberal professions, employees in establishments with more than five workers, and workers in the public sector) and domestic servants (most of whom were females). Just over 31 per cent of Belo Horizonte's active population were informal on that definition. Among working male heads of households, 15 per cent were informals concentrated in the youngest (14-19 years) and oldest (65+) age groups; among other male household members, 27 per cent were informals. Women were more heavily represented among the informals: 47 per cent of working female household heads, 36 per cent of spouses, 24 per cent of other female household members, and 100 per cent (by definition) of female domestic servants.

Merrick makes the point that supplemental earnings from the informal sector "represent an important element in the economic welfare, if not survival, of lower-income families". Earnings differentials between formal and informal are due partly to differences in educational levels but also partly to institutional arrangements: in the Belo Horizonte sample of households, earnings of individuals who have not completed primary school were considerably higher among the formals than among the informals for both men and women. Merrick found that the informal sector provided much of the employment and earnings opportunities available to the poorer households.

b. Cali (Colombia), 1976

Chris Birbeck examined recycling of waste materials out of the city garbage dump of Cali in 1976[31] as an example of a system of subcontracting between the formal and informal sectors built on the "illusion of independence" of the self-employed garbage pickers in what

Birkbeck categorises as a factory which lets "the large scale consumers of waste materials avoid having to accept some of their social responsibilities" as set out in existing labour legislation. The linkages to formal sector establishments on the output side were striking: waste paper and cardboard were processed to make tissues, cardboard and asphalted cardboard roofing tiles; recuperated tin and other metals were used by the foundries and steel works in Cali; and recuperated bottles were used by the state-owned liquor factory in Cali as well as by local laboratories and cosmetic firms.

c. Buenos Aires (Argentina), 1980

A sample survey of 854 self-employed and heads of micro-enterprises in Buenos Aires was carried out in 1980 for the ILO and the Government of Argentina under the direction of Jacques Delons[32]. The survey came at a time of economic stagnation in Argentina during which the proportion of wage and salary workers in the labour force was declining and the proportion of self-employed was rising. The sample was chosen from an existing list of self-employed individuals and small proprietors included in a sample designed for use by the permanent household survey of the Argentine Instituto Nacional de Estadistica y Censos. The bulk but not all could be considered informal. Of the sample, one per cent was in the primary sector, 20 per cent were in manufacturing, 11 per cent in construction, 41 per cent in commerce, 6 per cent in transport, 4 per cent in finance, and 17 per cent in other services; 30 per cent were women among whom 56 per cent were in commerce. Enterprise heads constituted 73 per cent of the sample; own account workers as such constituted the other 27 per cent. The self-employed and small proprietors were in general older than other components of the working population. Average income was higher for enterprise heads than for own-account workers, and higher for men than for women. By age group, average income was highest for those 40 to 49 years old. Two-thirds of the self-employed and small proprietors worked over 45 hours per week. Education levels were quite high: less than 0.5 per cent had no schooling, 18 per cent had incomplete primary schooling, 43 per cent had finished primary school, 17 per cent had incomplete middle schooling, 13 per cent had finished middle school, 5 per cent had incomplete university education and 4 per cent had finished university. By skill level, 9 per cent of the sample were professionals, 51 per cent were skilled, and 40 per cent were unskilled. As would be expected, average incomes increased with level of skill and with level of education.

Interestingly enough only 7 per cent of the sample gave scarcity of work opportunities in the wage sector as their principal reason for being self-employed; the largest group (35 per cent) cited expectation of higher incomes as their principal reason. The other categories were the desire to be independent (21 per cent), better possibility of using acquired skills (10 per cent), greater prestige (1 per cent), extra-economic factors such as distance, work time and family obligations (12 per cent), other (14 per cent).

Of the sample, 75 per cent operated from a fixed place of business, 9 per cent were itinerant, and 17 per cent worked at home. Those born in greater Buenos Aires made up 49 per cent of the sample, 38 per cent were migrants with twenty or more years of residence in greater Buenos Aires, 11 per cent were migrants with five to nineteen years of residence and only 2 per cent had less than five years of residence.

Of the sample, 39 per cent started business with their own capital, 4 per cent participated with partners, 4 per cent used severance compensation from a previous job, 14 per cent got loans from friends, relatives or other private sources, 4 per cent started with suppliers' credits, 4 per cent got loans from banks or credit co-operatives, 15 per cent already had all the necessary elements in hand, another 1 per cent used other unspecified sources, and 15 per cent needed no resources.

The bulk (75 per cent) of the sample sold their goods and services directly to consumers, 15 per cent to intermediaries, and the other 10 per cent directly to one or more enterprises on order. Methods of price fixing were the following: 12 per cent consulted their colleagues, 13 per cent tried to keep up with inflation, 19 per cent bargained with the customer, 19 per cent sold articles whose prices were fixed from outside (e.g. pharmaceuticals), 31 per cent added a fixed percentage to cost-price, and 6 per cent followed other procedures.

d. Mexico City (Mexico), 1981-82

Lourdes Beneria interviewed representatives of 67 firms of different sizes and different industries in Mexico City in 1981 and 1982 to identify the steps in the process of subcontracting to households[33]. Beneria is of the school that defines informality as the lack of adherence to legal regulations rather than as a question of size of enterprise, nature of production, or form of management; and subcontracting as a system for shifting employment toward the more informal (or underground) segments of the economy as a way to avoid state regulations on production and marketing, union contracts, and taxes, and to increase flexibility to expand and contract production. Beneria's study identified three patterns of articulation between the formal (legal, regulated) sector and the informal (illegal, unregulated) sector: direct articulation with no intermediaries; mediated articulation with a jobber as intermediary; and mixed articulation where a small enterprise combines legal and underground operations. An example of subcontracting that involved up to four levels of articulation was a multinational employing 3 000 workers that subcontracted out 70 per cent of its production to medium or smaller-scale firms from a list of 300 regulars and 1 500 occasionals. A medium scale-firm with Mexican capital employing 350 workers subcontracted out 5 per cent to small and micro-scale enterprises. A sweatshop operating illegally in the basement of the owner's residence and employing three workers at the legal minimum wage but with no fringe benefits, subcontracted out part of its production to homeworkers (the fourth level) at one-third the minimum wage. Homeworkers are mostly women.

e. Guadalajara (Mexico), 1982-85

Bryan Roberts' report on "ongoing research into urban poverty, the informal sector, and labor markets" in Guadalajara[34] referred to a labour market survey of some 800 workers from firms of different sizes and different types, a survey of an additional 500 workers in construction and some government agencies, case studies of some unregistered enterprises, interviews of 32 workers in those enterprises, and a neighbourhood-based sample survey of 100 low-income families. Roberts identified informal sector activities as those that "elude government requirements such as registration, tax and social security obligations, and health and safety rules ... often illegal, but not necessarily clandestine". Since the focus was on labour market status rather than on the status of an economic sector as such, employment was considered informal if it "is carried out without work contracts or with purely temporary ones, and payment is often by piece rate rather than by a fixed wage". On that criterion, Roberts found that in manufacturing the proportions of personnel not covered by social security and who had at best a purely temporary contract were as follows:

Size of enterprise (Number of workers)	Percentage informal
1-25	39
26-50	41
51-100	32
101-500	29
501 and over	20

Roberts added temporary workers not covered by social security to the self-employed and those working in unregistered enterprises to arrive at a total of informal workers equal to 40 or 42 per cent of the labour force in manufacturing in Guadalajara. Small workshops were more likely than large factories to employ their workers informally but 39 per cent of workers in firms with 20 or less had secure contracts. Informal employment (on Roberts' definition) varied by branch of activity: in the food industry, which is subject to marked seasonal variations, the proportion of temporary workers was higher in the larger firms (34 per cent) than in the smaller (28 per cent); in footwear manufacture, the reverse was the case (17 per cent in large firms and 48 per cent in small firms). Construction activity is also heavily seasonal (and cyclical) so that temporary contracts without welfare benefits were the norm rather than the exception. Younger workers tended to be informally employed (on Roberts' definition) but older males were likely to lose their jobs in manufacturing and to become self-employed or casual workers. Women were more likely (54 per cent) to be informally employed than men (36 per cent).

Informal employment was as frequent in the aggregate among natives of Guadalajara as migrants but the informal share varied from branch to branch. Natives were more prevalent than migrants in small workshops such as shoe manufacturing whereas migrants predominated in construction and construction materials. Income differences between formal and informal employment were not large, and in some branches such as footwear a skilled worker on piece rate could earn more than a worker in a large factory. Income differences were significant, within the informal sector, between owners of small workshops and their employees.

On Roberts' definition of informality, most enterprises in Guadalajara, including the largest multinationals, operated both formally and informally. Most households in Guadalajara had both formal and informal sector members. The two-generation household together with immediate kin and neighbourhood relationships were important elements for urban survival.

f. Montevideo (Uruguay) 1983-84

A 1983-84 survey of 700 households in low-income districts of Montevideo, carried out as part of a CIESU-Johns Hopkins University study on the informal sector in Uruguay[35], found that 35 per cent of the households were involved in informal activities as self-employed or as wage-workers or as employers, with informality defined as participation in the labour force without access to social security benefits. The informals so defined constituted 34 per cent of artisans and production workers, 27 per cent of those in personal services and 26 per cent of vendors. Females made up 46 per cent of the informals in services and 23 per cent in trade.

The Montevideo study also identified significant linkages between formal and informal sector activities in two branches of activity: footwear manufacturing and recycling of waste materials. Footwear manufacturing involves a range of institutional arrangements on the border between legality and illegality. Some shops employing wage labour are legal but also employ clandestine labour; others are underground. Some shops employing mainly family workers also employ clandestine wage-workers. Other producers work at home at piece rates (at levels of physical productivity higher than among factory operatives). Recycling of waste materials involves three stages of activity: collecting and sorting; cleaning and processing; and marketing. At each stage the wholesalers and factories rely primarily on household workers to keep labour costs low.

g. Lima (Peru) in the 1980s according to Hernando de Soto

Hernando de Soto's well-known book on *The Other Path (El Otro Sendero)* defines informality in relation to legality. Informal activity is desirable and productive economic activity carried on outside the law (because the law is not adapted to economic realities); it is to be distinguished from undesirable and counter-productive criminal activity (e.g. the drug trade) also carried on outside the law. De Soto's informality is not necessarily related to size of the enterprise concerned, although the informal enterprise will usually be small. De Soto's thesis is that the informals are entrepreneurs operating outside, or on the fringes, of the law because the laws and regulations have been designed to limit entry to formal business status and access to property rights. His proposed antidote to underdevelopment is to open the gates of legality to the informals and thereby to unleash their entrepreneurial energies.

The first part of de Soto's book is a description of the process by which the informals have infiltrated and finally overwhelmed the city of Lima in housing, commerce, and passenger transport during the last half-century. Pushed into town by population growth in rural areas and pulled by the opening up of highways, the rural emigrants have vastly extended the boundaries of the colonial city with the establishment of increasing numbers of peripheral settlements, most of them by illegal invasions of public (and in some cases private) land. They have sought to support themselves initially by street vending and then by creating off-street markets. The informals invaded the streets with collective taxis and minibuses to provide transport inside the town for established city dwellers, and for the newly urbanized commuters from the peripheral settlements into town. The book also discusses informal sector industrial activity, which has grown rapidly in small units and "underground" in order to avoid detection, but the main focus is on housing, commerce and transport which are very visible and very much above ground.

A major emphasis of de Soto's book is on the development of the extralegal system regulating relationships among the informals - in establishing and developing housing settlements, in the acquisition and sale of quasi-property rights of street vendors to space in the streets and in off-street markets created by former street vendors, and in the allocation of minibus routes in and out of the city. All three of those activities require the agreement of many participants on rules governing social and business behaviour; the informal rules are adhered to because they are relevant to day-to-day coexistence with neighbours, business competitors, customers and suppliers whereas the formal body of laws and regulations is virtually ignored or by-passed.

De Soto gives a number of examples of how the extralegal system functions. Because of the virtual impossibility of legally acquiring land for settlement, the collective invasion of public land has been developed as the major form of land acquisition for housing, to the point where false invasions to private land are organized in collusion with landowners threatened by expropriation and false invasions of public land are organized by the government itself in order to cut through otherwise impenetrable forests of red tape. Street vendors establish sales routes in competition and in cooperation with others while they are still itinerant peddlers, and gradually acquire quasi-property rights to a fixed location for sales on the street. Once established, the location has a sales value (and can indeed be bought and sold); it can be shared by vendors of different commodities depending on the time of day or night; and it can be protected against other invaders and the police by direct collective action (or by indirect political action in cooperation with an interested politician in need of votes). Eventually the vendors struggle to get off the street and to establish collective mini-markets where they can acquire relative stability and space for storage as well as the critical mass needed to draw customers to them from the street.

Lima's informal urban transport system has virtually displaced the formal system in part because of the government's attempts to impose price controls which drove the formal bus companies into bankruptcy. The informals competed with the formal bus companies on existing routes and established new routes to meet new needs. In the process, they have had to work out new cooperative arrangements among themselves; but competition is keen, vehicle maintenance is poor, drivers are undisciplined, and accident rates are high.

In developing his view that reform of the structure of law is the key to economic development, de Soto cites a number of horror stories on the obstructive nature of existing regulations: that legal adjudication of undeveloped state land requires a minimum of 56 months of effort and the completion of 207 administrative steps involving 48 public offices, and an additional 27 months to obtain a licence to develop the land and build on it; that 9 years and 8 months are required for complying with bureaucratic steps involved for informal street vendors to construct markets or commercial centers; that it took 289 days working 6 hours a day to complete the formalities necessary to open a ficticious small garment factory with two sewing machines.

D. Survey Conclusions: Perceptions of Informal Sector Behaviour

The surveys in Africa, Asia and Latin America reported in this chapter illustrate a variety of types of informal sector behaviour and a variety of perceptions of it by academic and other researchers. Most of the field surveys have been carried out in Africa whereas most of the theorizing has been done in Latin America. The approach in Asia has been largely pragmatic. The casual empiricism of the 1972 ILO Kenya Employment Mission has been reinforced and amplified by the considerable number of systematic field surveys cited above (and others whose results were not available to the author): there have been shifts in focus and in emphasis, but the general picture of informal sector activities sketched for Kenya in 1972 still has a remarkable resemblance to what has been identified in an increasing number of countries of the Third World since then.

The similarities among the many cases cited earlier in this chapter stem from the prevailing demographic trends (high population growth rates and high rural to urban migration rates and the world wide economic stagnation of the 1980s. Informal sector activities absorb between 40 and 60 per cent of the urban labour force of many of the Third World cities studied. Within the informal sector, petty trade is the predominant activity, but informal sector producers of goods and services provide a substantial supplement to (and compete vigorously with) the goods and services supplied by the formal sector. Informal sector enterprise heads (both artisans and traders) often earn more than the official minimum wage or the average wage in the formal sector; informal sector employees usually earn less than the official minimum wage. Informal sector artisans and traders provide on-the-job training to the bulk of the informal sector labour force, often as the only substitute for educational facilities that are not available to the children of the working poor coming from both rural and urban areas.

Backward linkages to formal sector suppliers of inputs are strong; forward linkages are generally limited to households and other informal sector producers.

The differences among the cases stem from differences in general levels of technology and in levels of industrialization. The availability to informal sector producers of functional second hand machinery is much greater in Buenos Aires and in Madras where there is an active indigenous industrial sector than in Togo or Dakar. Similarly, forward linkages to formal sector producers through subcontracts are likely to come into existence only beyond a certain threshold of industrialization, although formal sector distributors can be efficient market intermediaries for goods (such as metal or wooden furniture) produced by informal sector artisans.

Most of the studies sponsored by the international and bilateral aid agencies have focused on the potentially viable micro-enterprises that constitute George Nihan's "modern informal sector". Some of the university-generated studies, particularly those by the radical economists, have on occasion been more concerned with the ostensibly marginal activities such as garbage reprocessing and lottery ticket selling that also form part of the informal sector. It should be noted in passing, however, that the Third World's biggest informal garbage collection system, the collection of Cairo's solid waste by the *zabaleen* of Fustat and their donkeys, has been the focus of a major World Bank urban improvement project.

The most significant recent change in emphasis has been the shift from the micro-enterprise as such to the regulatory framework that encourages informal sector micro-enterprises to stay small. Avoidance of government regulations and taxes was one of the characteristics of informality originally specified in the definition formulated by the ILO

Kenya Employment Mission Report of 1972, but informality has taken on a new dimension since the publication of Hernando de Soto's *The Other Path* in 1986. The new wave of research on the informal sector may be described as an examination of the comptability between regulations and growth of small and micro-scale enterprise activity, with a view to reforming the regulatory framework.

Notes and References

1. ILO, (1972).
2. JOSHI, LUBELL and MOULY (1973). Quantitative estimates were derived from Société d'Etudes Economiques et Financières (1973).
3. SETHURAMAN (1981c).
4. SETHURAMAN (1974).
5. FOWLER (1981), FAPOHUNDA (1981), MABOGUNJE and FILANI (1981); and ARYEE (1981).
6. GERRY (1974).
7. NIHAN, DVIRY and JOURDAIN (1978); and NIHAN and JOURDAIN (1978).
8. NIHAN, DEMOL, DVIRY and JONDOH (1978); and NIHAN, DEMOL and JONDOH (1979).
9. NIHAN, JOURDAIN and SIDIBE (1979).
10. NIHAN, DVIRY and SCHWARTZ (1978).
11. NIHAN, DEMOL and TABI (1982); and DEMOL and NIHAN (1982). See also MALDONADO, DEMOL and CAPT (1987).
12. ZAROUR (1989) and LUBELL and ZAROUR (1990).
13. CESM (1976).
14. HOUSE (1987).
15. ILO/Jobs and Skills Programme for Africa (JASPA) (1985). See also VAN DIJK (1986).
16. GOZO (1988).
17. HOUSE (1984).
18. TOURE (1987).
19. SETHURAMAN (1981c).
20. AMIN (1987).
21. ILO/ARTEP (1988).
22. NATIONAL INSTITUTE OF URBAN AFFAIRS (1987).
23. LALL (1987).
24. SETHURAMAN (1981c). See also OFISEL Ltda. (1977), LUBELL and MCCALLUM (1978), BERLINK et al. (1981), and SANCHEZ et al. (1981).
25. SOUZA and TOKMAN (1976), pp. 396-397.
26. TOKMAN (1978), p. 313.
27. TOKMAN, (1990).
28. PREALC (1978): Part III, El Sector Informal en Algunas Ciudades: chapter 1, Asuncion; chapter 2, Ciudad de Mexico, Guadalajara y Monterrey; chapter 3, San Salvador; chapter 4, Quito y Guayaquil; chapter 5, Kingston. Part IV, Casos de Actividades Informales: chapter 1, El Comercio en Pequena Escala en San Salvador; chapter 2, El Comercio de Alimentos en Santiago.
29. PREALC (1988). See also TOKMAN (1978a).

30. MERRICK (1976).
31. BIRKBECK (1978).
32. REPUBLICA ARGENTINA (1981).
33. BENERIA (1989).
34. ROBERTS (1989).
35. FORTUNA and PRATES (1989). See also PORTES, BLITZER and CURTIS (1986).
36. DE SOTO (1989) and (1986) and DE SOTO (1988).

Chapter 3

POLICIES FOR THE INFORMAL SECTOR

Policies proposed for dealing with informal sector activities have taken several tracks. Most of the international agencies involved have been concerned with the informal sector because of their interest in employment creation or poverty alleviation. Governments have been of two minds, sometimes simultaneously: they want to encourage productive micro-enterprise activity, but they also want to control it, to limit its geographical range of activity in the cities, and to tax it. The attitudes of both the governments and the international agencies toward the informal sector are essentially reformist: they believe that the positive role played in the national economy by the informal sector can be enhanced by changes in policies at the macroeconomic level and at the enterprise level. The Marxist academics on the other hand take a negatively critical view of the whole informal sector phenomenon. They focus on its exploitative aspects and see little hope of improvement through policy change until the "system", however they define it (capitalism, neo-colonialism, indigenous state capitalism, domination of the periphery by the north Atlantic and north Pacific "centre"), is washed away.

A. Recommendations of the ILO Kenya Employment Mission Report

The 1972 ILO Kenya Employment Mission[1] sketched out the main contours of a coherent policy package for promotion of informal sector activities. The policy package had two main themes: reducing the risks and uncertainties to which informal sector operators are subject; and to establishing links between the formal and informal sectors. Since most of the risks were due to harassment by the government authorities, the main plea of the Kenya report was for a positive attitude on the part of the government toward promotion of the informal sector. Specifically, the ILO team called on the authorities: to cease demolition of informal sector housing except where the squatter-built land was genuinely required for housing development and town planning purposes; to eliminate unnecessary trade and commercial licensing and to substitute health and safety inspection for licensing; to issue licenses to any applicant able to pay the license fee; to intensify technical research and development on products suitable for informal sector production or use; to orient government purchasing and construction contracts toward informal sector enterprises where possible; to speed up payments on government contracts by substituting direct payments for the government purchase order system and to increase the preference margin for local suppliers on government contracts; to use industrial estates for promoting subcontracting and to induce larger firms to train local subcontractors.

Sethuraman carried those themes further in his work on the informal sector for the ILO in Geneva[2], emphasizing the importance of increasing access by the informal sector to factors of production and to markets: access to improved skills, access to credit, access to suitable infrastructure and market locations, access to improved technology (especially in manufacturing), access to raw materials, access to government contracts, and access to formal sector subcontracting. Removing licensing and zoning restrictions on informal sector activity at the local level is a relatively passive element of the policy package. The other elements call for positive interventions: reorienting formal and informal training facilities to improve and supplement traditional apprenticeship systems; changing bank lending procedures to take into account the needs and absorptive capacity of informal sector participants; incorporation of market facilities into physical urban planning and encouragement of auto-construction of business premises through the provision of cheap building materials and advice; active encouragement of technology transfer and the development of appropriate technology; intervention in the market to ease shortages of traditional raw materials (leather, wood, metals) and training in the use of substitute materials (vinyl, plastic materials); modifying government contracting procedures; and active encouragement of subcontracting arrangements between formal and informal sector producers.

B. The PREALC Policy Position

The ILO's Regional Employment Program for Latin America and the Caribbean (PREALC) devoted considerable effort to the formulation of policy recommendations for the informal sector under the direction of Victor Tokman. Reflecting the ILO's concern with employment and poverty in the mid-1970s, PREALC prescribed three types of measures to increase productivity and total income of the informal sector: those aimed at increasing the sector's economic efficiency; those aimed at increasing its production; and those aimed at shifting people out of saturated activities with no possibility of expansion into activities with better prospects[3]. In the PREALC view, the small scale of informal sector production was a major reason for its relative inefficiency as compared with that of the modern sector. Some of the negative effects of the small scale of production could be offset by organising co-operatives or similar institutions to reduce marketing costs, and by making credit available to informal sector producers by creating a lending institution devoted specially to informal sector borrowers and establishing appropriate procedures for making loans. Such an institution should be endowed with the necessary resources and should have appropriate procedures for making loans to informal sector borrowers. Scientific and technical institutes should focus on the development and spread of technology appropriate to increasing the productivity and improving the products of the informal sector. Measures for training informal sector participants should include components on the organisation and management of small enterprises.

With regard to policies for expanding the markets for informal sector production, it was the PREALC view that account must be taken of existing relationships of competition and complementarity between the informal and formal sectors. Some of the competitive advantages of the formal sector may be due to special treatment by the political authorities in the form of subsidies, credit facilities and other government incentives to which the informal sector does not have access; such distortions could be removed. On the positive side, subcontracting by the formal sector to informal sector enterprises could be reinforced by organising subcontracting pools and by directing government purchases toward the informal sector for products where informal sector suppliers are important. The government could also subsidise infrastructure used by the informal sector, for example by the construction of public markets. Larger firms that subcontract-out work could assist informal sector producers by providing funds, machinery, quality control, new designs and training[4]. Informal sector producers could be organised for merchandising of their output for export. Reservation of markets for small-scale producers could be used as a policy instrument.

Access by informal sector producers to bank credit could be facilitated by providing special lines of credit through the banks with provision for increasing the banker's spread to offset higher costs of administering loans to informal sector producers, for providing risk insurance for loans to micro-enterprises, and for re-insuring loans with organisations of informal sector producers. Programmes for increasing the qualifications of informal sector participants should take into account the important constraint that time spent being trained usually implies time lost from an income-earning activity and may involve other costs for transportation and subsistence. One proposal made by PREALC was to combine unemployment subsidies with training; another was to give incentives to small enterprises to increase their training activities in the work place.

Application of the policy instruments cited above implied, for PREALC, an increase in the role of the state even if a great deal of additional resources is not required. It also implies greater participation of informal sector participants in the policy decision-making process.

The elements of the PREALC policy prescription were restated in the mid-1980s in a study on the informal sector in Central America: improving access to factors of production; raising the level of technology; stimulating demand; organising and grouping small enterprises; and modifying the legal and institutional framework[5]. In order to facilitate access by informal sector enterprises to raw material inputs and machinery, the report recommended establishing a distribution network to lower the prices paid by micro-enterprises and reducing tariffs on imported capital goods and intermediate goods used only by micro-enterprises. (Neither of the two recommendations looks viable: there is little likelihood that a purchasing agency for the informal sector will be more efficient than, and therefore competitive with, the existing commercial intermediaries, or that the authorities can distinguish between goods destined for use by the informal sector and those for use by the formal sector.) A third suggestion was for the government to subsidise the creation of infrastructure (markets and work places) for informal sector participants.

Policies to raise the technological level of informal sector producers would include the provision of loans for purchasing capital goods that incorporate more modern technologies, the initiation of programmes for training to use the new equipment, and efforts to create improved designs that would increase customer acceptance of informal sector outputs. Policies to stimulate demand for goods and services produced by the informal sector would include construction of market places, organisation of promotional fairs for small producers, issue of more permits for street sellers of informal sector products, prospecting for export markets, and the reservation of certain markets (as in India) for micro-enterprise production or micro-enterprise commerce (e.g. sale of fresh fruits and vegetables). Encouragement of organisations of informal sector producers would stop short of trying to create full producer co-operatives. Such efforts would most effectively be limited to the co-operative purchasing of inputs, selling of outputs, and provision of technical assistance. Modification of the legal and institutional framework would include: taking account of the special features of the informal sector in economic planning and in the design of legislation; consideration of the interaction between the general policy framework and policies for the informal sector; and the creation of an organisation for micro-enterprise development to evaluate policies, to prepare relevant legislation, and to try to harmonize the various programmes and projects for support of the informal sector.

In a recent article on the informal sector in Latin America for a symposium on expanding income opportunities for women in developing countries, Victor Tokman provided a further amplification of the three main elements of the PREALC policy approach: providing productive assistance to informal sector enterprises; giving support to informal sector participants; and revising the norms and regulations that affect informal sector activity[6]. Measures for providing productive assistance to informal sector producers would include eliminating restrictions that prevent informal sector enterprises from submitting bids on government contracts, and perhaps facilitating their participation in such bidding by facilitating access to credit through mechanisms such as trusts or insurance plans which deal with groups rather than individuals, and by training informal sector producers in accounting and managerial procedures. Welfare measures to help the poorest of the informals, such as greater access to improved health and educational facilities, would have a positive effect on households whose homes are also the place of work.

The legal-institutional package proposed by Tokman would distinguish between purely bureaucratic obstacles to achieving legality (which may or may not be enforced) and regulations designed to protect the general interests of the community. It would also distinguish between evasion of building standards and zoning laws by formal sector builders in medium- to high-income areas for their own financial convenience and disregard of unrealistic standards by builders of informal sector housing in shanty towns because of lack of economic resources.

With regard to taxes, Tokman pointed out that given the low levels of income and profits of informal sector participants, direct taxes are usually not relevant. However, the informal sector is affected by indirect taxes, particularly the value added tax. Fiscal policy-makers could exempt small commercial transactions from the value added tax. If informal sector producers are nevertheless subjected to the value added tax, the mechanism for deduction of payments at previous stages should be explained to them.

According to Tokman, most of the labour regulations in force in Latin America were designed for formal sector enterprises and are simply not applicable to the informal sector. Most micro-enterprises do not generate enough of a margin of profitability to afford payroll deductions to cover contributions to health and accident insurance; but such benefits for informal sector workers could be covered by the state out of general revenues as part of the general welfare budget. Benefits related to job security and pensions assume long-term employment in formal sector enterprises; in view of the basic insecurity of informal sector activity, the reasonable approach is simply to exempt informal sector producers from the unemployment and pension components of the regulations.

In Tokman's view, his proposals add up to a programme for improving the efficiency of government intervention by rationalising it in some cases, reducing or eliminating it in others, and increasing it in still others; they are not intended to generate new institutions or additional bureaucracy.

In another recent article[7], Tokman warns of the risks in designing policy for the informal sector. The first risk is the temptation to find "the missing piece" of the policy puzzle without recognising the importance of other factors. A second is to fail to consider the heterogeneity of the informal sector and of the interests of different groups within it. Another is to ignore the significance of different forms of production (e.g. the household as workplace which facilitates family labour participation but which also makes it possible to combine welfare with productive policies). The policymaker's task is to identify the relevant policy instruments and levels of intervention in the light of those risks.

C. Hernando de Soto's Invisible Revolution

Hernando de Soto's central policy prescription for Peru[8] (and, by implication, for other countries of Latin America) is to remove government restrictions on freedom of entry of micro-enterprises into productive activity and to abolish unnecessary licensing requirements and absurd bureaucratic approval procedures: government should, to the greatest extent possible, remove itself from the market place and leave informal sector participants free to use their energies to create the goods and services the economy demands. Unlike PREALC, de Soto sees little or no positive role for government in dealing with the informal sector. There would seem, however, to be limits to the effectiveness of the de Soto approach.

For example, in describing the process of organising land invasions and the development of informal housing settlements, de Soto seems to imply that easier access to property rights would directly resolve the problem of urban housing for the unending flow of rural to urban migrants. However, the level of rural to urban migration, which results from population growth and the lack of economic opportunities in the countryside, is so high that it will continue to overwhelm absorption capacity of the city even if the system of assigning property rights is drastically liberalised. Similarly, de Soto's prescription for getting peddlers off the streets of Lima, which is to help them build informal markets, is not likely to reduce the pressure on the main thoroughfares of downtown Lima as long as the inflow of migrants is as high as it is. Since the main streets of the city are where the highest number of potential customers throng, demand for entry by vendors will continue to exceed the available space for sales locations for a long time to come, independently of the availability of space in off-street markets. By the same token, there will always be pressure of informal transport operators on the streets of and leading to the central city until saturation of the routes drives prices down to below operating costs of the formals. Victor Tokman makes this same point in his article on "Policies for a Heterogeneous Informal Sector in Latin America"[6]: "... there is little to be done with such clearly overflowing sectors as street peddling. Although transitory measures will alter the situation temporarily, sooner or later it will recur, since it exists because of a semipermanent structural labor surplus that will decrease only when sufficient productive employment has been generated". There is, nevertheless, a possible safety valve in the broader implication of de Soto's argument that generally easier access to legal (formal) business status and to full property rights will cause an overall expansion of economic activity and that economic growth will expand the economic capacity of the city to absorb the expanding labour force into productive activities other than street vending and informal transport services.

De Soto is clearly on the right track in distinguishing between "good laws" that guarantee and promote economic efficiency and "bad laws" that protect a privileged minority by restricting access to urban housing and economic activity and thereby impede and disrupt economic efficiency. De Soto calls for the design and adoption of "facilitative legal instruments" (impartially adjudicated contract, property and torts law) to assure firm property rights, reliable transactions and secure activities, and for the avoidance of obstructive legal norms.

De Soto proposes an "agenda for change" that would adjust existing legal institutions drawing on the extralegal system within which the informal sector now regulates property rights and contracts. According to de Soto, "the spontaneous generation of extralegal norms by the informals has initiated a reform of the *status quo*, pointing the way that legal institutions must go if they are to adapt to new circumstances and regain social relevance". He proposes simplication, decentralisation and deregulation (or depoliticisation) of national economic life. Simplification implies identifying and eliminating legislation that raises the costs of entering and remaining in formal activity. Specifically, de Soto's Instituto Libertad y Democracia has proposed a freedom of information law for Peru to open up legislation to public strutiny, and a housing construction title law simplifying the process of certifying home ownership. Decentralisation implies transferring legislative and administrative responsibilities from the central government to local and regional governments and other bodies that are likely to be closer to the realities on the ground than is the central government. Deregulation implies increasing the responsibilities and opportunities of private individuals and reducing those of the state, in particular by removing from the hands of the state "the power to decide who can produce and who cannot, what goods and services will be authorised, how they will be produced, and at what prices and in what quantities", a view with which few would nowadays disagree.

D. The Macro-Economic Policy Environment

The differing effects of macroeconomic policies on large enterprises and on small and micro-enterprises have been summarised by Carl Liedholm and Donald Mead[9] according to policy impacts on input markets and on product output markets. Policy instruments affecting capital inputs (such as subsidised credit, balance-of-payments regulations based on an overvalued exchange rate combined with import duties and import quotas, and capital-oriented tax incentives) have been biased in favour of large enterprises and against small enterprises by reducing the cost of capital to large enterprises. Even interest rate ceilings, the one policy instrument aimed at protecting small borrowers, have had as their main result a reduction in lending to small enterprises. Similarly, larger firms have benefited from tariff reductions and the subsidy created by an overvalued exchange rate on direct imports of raw material inputs, advantages that have not been available to informal sector producers. Policy instruments affecting labour inputs (in particular minimum wage legislation, mandated fringe benefits and other labour regulations, and public sector wage policy) have resulted in increased wage costs in formal sector enterprises. Informal sector and other small enterprises have often been able to avoid enforcement of such measures thereby enabling them to stay in business by keeping their labour costs down. Attempts by government authorities to enforce compliance by informal sector enterprises with wage legislation and labour regulations threaten one of the few cost advantages available to the informal sector. On the output side, foreign trade policy has also discriminated against small and micro-enterprises. As evidence Liedholm and Mead cite estimates showing that sectors where large-scale enterprises predominate have tended to have positive (and relatively high) rates of effective protection while sectors where small-scale enterprises predominate have low or negative rates of effective protection. In some countries, eligibility for export subsidies has been limited to enterprises exporting more than a certain minimum value, which again discriminates against the smallest producers.

The macroeconomic structural adjustment measures implemented by a number of developing countries during the 1980s have reduced some of the discrimination against small and micro-enterprises discussed above. Currency devaluations (in countries other than those of the franc currency zone in Africa), reductions in quantitative restrictions, and revision of import tariff structures have reduced the implicit import subsidies to capital and raw material inputs of the earlier trade regimes. Large size of firm remains an advantage in access to lower cost inputs, by virtue of bargaining power and the ability to purchase in bulk, but the additional advantages of large size resulting from earlier macroeconomic policy distortions have been reduced. At the same time, increases in interest rate ceilings for loans to small enterprises are becoming acceptable, so there is some hope of increased availability of credit for small enterprises.

The spread of informality (defined as avoidance of regulations) into the operations of formal sector business, which is most evident in subcontracting arrangements in the newly industrialising countries of Latin America and elsewhere[10], creates a certain tension in government attitudes toward the informal sector: closing an eye to tax evasion and violation of labour regulations on the part of very small and micro-enterprises is a way of promoting employment, encouraging production and generating incomes; but letting avoidance of taxes and regulations spread too far undermines the legitimacy of the corpus of social legislation and social accomplishments of the past several decades. At what size of firm to impose strict enforcement is now becoming a serious question.

The policy tension is at its most evident in regard to taxation. Many, if not most, of the micro-enterprises of the informal sector survive by "exploiting" themselves and their family workers, probably by exploiting their apprentices, and usually by avoiding taxes where they can manage to do so. Governments, once sensitised to the economic importance of the informal sector, are torn between the desirability of promoting informal sector activity and the finance ministry's reflex to extend the tax net as far as it can. The tax collector's reflex is particularly strong where, as in some countries of francophone Africa, formal sector activity is stagnating or declining and with it the country's habitual tax base; but giving free rein to that reflex is eminently short-sighted.

E. Micro-Level Policy Interventions

Most of the efforts of governments and aid agencies to support informal sector activity have in fact gone into micro-level interventions, as will be described in chapter 4 below, aimed at providing credit and extension services to the more viable of the population of micro and small enterprises[11]. The policy instruments used have included the provision of credit on preferential terms, management and marketing assistance, technical assistance in product design and production methods, vocational training, and assistance in establishing new enterprises. Benefits have mostly been limited to the small minority of enterprises directly touched by projects using such micro-level instruments, since the projects are too small to reach the mass of their potential targeted clientele. In addition, the projects usually ignore the vast majority of marginal and presumably non-viable activities outside the target group, hoping for additional social welfare measures to promote direct poverty alleviation.

F. Not So Benign Neglect: Africa and Asia

Government policy toward the informal sector in Africa and Asia has focused more on controlling micro-enterprise activity that encumbers the streets of the major cities than on developing the productive potentialities of the informal sector. At best, governments are in two minds about how to deal with informal sector activity. They are aware of its productive attributes but they want to keep it out of sight. The typical reaction is that of the authorities in Jakarta who intermittently harass street traders but who also have been making some effort to create marketplaces for traders following recommendations of the ILO and the World Bank's urban project experts. India, whose concern with promoting cottage industries dates back to the Gandhian movement, is an exception, although even in India promotion of informal sector activity is not very high on the list of the government's operational programmes. The official attitude in Senegal is typical of the new awareness in Africa: the agency concerned with employment creation is actively looking for ways to promote informal sector activity; the Ministry of Finance is looking for ways to tax it.

G. Benign Neglect: The OECD Countries and Eastern Europe

According to all reports, northern Italy's industrial economy is flourishing on the basis of the quasi-informality that goes with avoidance of regulations and taxes. Such quasi-informality (the "grey" economy) makes it possible to cut costs for production and export and meets with the tacit approval of the authorities. In the United States, pockets of quasi-informal sector activity have developed in the Chinese and Cuban immigrant communities which have recreated the sweatshops that were the bane of the American garment workers unions earlier in the 20th century. The US Departement of Labour makes some efforts to enforce existing labour legislation but it is also aware that the sweatshops reduce unemployment.

The new economic liberalism in Eastern Europe is transforming into petty capitalism what used to be considered black market activity. It will be particularly interesting for the informal sector watcher to follow the development of Eastern Europe's quasi-informal sector during the transition of economic policy from central planning to relatively unfettered market economics.

Notes and References

1. ILO (1972).
2. SETHURAMAN (1981c).
3. SOUZA and TOKMAN (1976).
4. TOKMAN (1978b).
5. HAAN (1985), Chapter 5.
6. TOKMAN (1989).
7. TOKMAN (1990).
8. DE SOTO (1989).
9. LIEDHOLM and MEAD (1987).
10. PORTES, CASTELLS and BENTON (1989).
11. LEE (1987).

Chapter 4

PROGRAMMES IN SUPPORT OF INFORMAL SECTOR ACTIVITIES

Programmes in support of parts of the informal sector, particularly artisanal or micro-enterprise activities, have been in operation since long before the informal sector label was invented, but increased awareness of the productive capacities of the informal sector has intensified national government and international agency interest in expanding and improving existing programmes and in developing new ones. This chapter reviews some of the programmes that have been proposed and implemented since the early 1970s.

The elements of the various programmes are the five types of assistance to small (and micro) enterprises cited by Carl Liedholm and Donald Mead[1]: credit; technical and production assistance; management assistance; marketing assistance; and common facilities. The forms of assistance and delivery channels used by assistance projects for each of these types of assistance are summarised in Table 4.1 below.

In reviewing a wide range of assistance projects and evaluations of them, Liedholm and Mead found that most such projects had a credit component and that most proprietors perceive capital (primarily working capital) to be their most pressing input constraint, but that working capital shortages are often symptomatic of other problems. Nevertheless, the record of success is good for assistance programmes whose credit component was applied to working capital. Non-financial assistance schemes have not been particularly successful in benefit-cost terms. Effective schemes were those that managed to open up a situation where only Peter Kilby's single "missing ingredient" was needed[2]. Schemes assisting existing enterprises were more likely to be successful than those attempting to establish new small enterprises; industrial estate schemes have typically not been effective because a considerable number of missing ingredients need to be provided at high cost.

A. Informal Sector Projects and the National Plan in Colombia

One of the first of the countries of the Third World to incorporate promotion of informal activities into its development plans and programmes as an explicit national goal was Colombia. In the wake of the 1970 report of the ILO Employment Mission to Colombia[3], all of Colombia's national plans published during the 1970s had employment as a central concern; by the late 1970s, the "so-called informal sector" was accepted as a significant locus of employment creation. The Plan de Integración Nacional 1979-1982 put aside any expectation of seeing the informal sector absorbed by the formal sector and tried to formulate a policy for promoting viable economic activities of the informal sector and for raising the productivity of those working in them[4]. A two-pronged approach was proposed:

Table 4.1

TYPES AND FORMS OF ASSISTANCE TO SMALL
AND MICRO-SCALE ENTERPRISES AND DELIVERY CHANNEL USED

Types of assistance	Forms of assistance	Delivery channels
Credit	Loans in cash and/or in kind, for fixed assets and/or for working capital	Commercial banks Specialized banks Finance corporations Extension agents Loan boards Cooperatives PVOs Informal channels
Technical and production assistance	Advice on processes, design of products, tools, equipment, machines, quality control, plant layout	Vocational training institutions Trade centres Extension services at industrial development centres or through mobile workshops Appropriate technology units PVOs Local entrepreneurs
Management assistance	Bookkeeping Accounting Auditing Production planning Inventory Personnel management Entrepreneurship development	Vocational training institutions Management development institutions Extension services at industrial centers or through mobile workshops Formal and informal meetings Newletters PVOs
Marketing assistance	Advice on packaging, merchandising, product demand Raw material procurement Emporia sales and displays at home and abroad Collection centers Sales on consignment Export service Credit insurance	Extension services Trading corporations Credit and export schemes Customer service centres Handicraft centres Display centres Cooperatives PVOs
Common facilities	Buildings Road Engineering workshops Electricity and water	Industrial estate areas or sites Workshop complexes Cooperatives

Source: Carl Liedholm and Donald Mead, *Small Scale Industries in Developing Countries: Empirical Evidence and Policy Implications*, East Lansing, Michigan State University, MSU Development Paper No. 9, 1987 quoting C. Chuta and Carl Liedholm, *Rural Non-Farm Employment: A Review of the State of the Art*, East Lansing, Michigan State University, MSU Development Paper No. 4, 1979.

a) to develop financial intermediation mechanisms that would take account of the special needs of the informal sector; and b) to encourage the transfer of technology to informal sector enterprises, improve the quality of enterprise management in the informal sector, and to arrive at better integration of informal sector producers into the market. The instruments proposed to facilitate credit intermediation were a guaranty fund to be financed by an interest surcharge, provision of soft loans to intermediate credit institutions in partial compensation for higher costs of administering loans to informal sector enterprises, and the use as financial intermediaries of special institutions attuned to providing credit and technical assistance to very small enterprises. The instruments proposed for direct assistance at the enterprise level were extension to the informal sector of the training and technical cooperation services of the Servicio Nacional de Aprendizaje (SENA), the adoption of legal measures to facilitate the creation of associations of small enterprises, and the rationalization of efforts to foster such associations on the basis of economic viability.

Colombia's National Integration Plan also proposed, as social policy for the informal sector, the gradual expansion of existing social service entities to cover informal sector participants. That would entail a) lowering the minimum number of workers and eliminating the minimum capital required for an enterprise to adhere to Colombia's social insurance funds (*cajas de compensación*) and b) orienting their health, nutrition and other benefits more toward low income groups (which presumably include many of the informals). Since the informals in non-viable activities would most likely remain poor, the plan also called for efforts to improve physical and social infrastructure facilities in urban districts where informal sector participants are concentrated. The Plan thus tried to distinguish between programmes intended to increase the productivity and incomes of informal sector participants and those intended to alleviate poverty through the provision of social services and social infrastructure.

In practice, attempts to implement the proposed programmes were far from successful. In Cali, informal sector producers resisted joining associations such as the chamber of commerce because membership would open them to the imposition of fees, taxes, and quotas. Attempts to organize community enterprises were made in Bogota and Cali starting in 1974. An organization called the Centro de Investigación y Educación Popular (CINEP) organized 15 such community enterprises on behalf of SENA but only one survived; the others fell apart because of personal conflicts or because the more successful individuals preferred working on their own. In 1975, the Fundacion Carvajal organized a conservative small enterprise development programme in Cali that combined the three elements of advice, training, and credit. The programme selected enterprises to be assisted in several steps: it carried out a barrio census of 3 700 micro-enterprises, chose 2 800 of them for a closer survey, and selected 800 as potential clients of the programme. Out of those, 180 submitted loan proposals of which 169 were approved for loans at 24 per cent annual interest. The programme followed the loan recipients closely and provided them with management advice, with relatively successful results. It did not solve the problem of how to assist the large majority of micro enterprises that did not appear particularly viable from the start.

B. Micro-Enterprise Projects in Latin America Supported by the Inter-American Development Bank

A variety of micro-enterprise support projects, most of them receiving financial support from the Inter-American Bank (IDB) through its Small Projects programme, were described in documents presented to the Seminar on Assistance to Micro-producers in Latin America held at the IDB in Washington, DC in February 1989[5].

One of the institutions represented was the Fundación Carvajal of Cali (Colombia) referred to in section 4.A above, which described its management training, advisory, and credit programmes for micro-enterprises. Between 1977 and 1988, the Fundación Carvajal had presented over 1 200 training courses with around 25 000 participants and had provided individualized advice to 5 500 micro-enterprises, 40 per cent of which also received loans amounting to over two million dollars. In 1987, a total of 725 loans were issued, 313 of which were second loans.

Guatemala's Programa Nacional de Microempresas Urbanas under the Vice-Presidency of the Republic has developed what it calls a Sistema Multiplicador de Microempresaries (SIMME) carried out through local private voluntary non-governmental organisations (NGOs). The SIMME has several components: an enterprise counselling service responsible for selecting micro-entrepreneurs, evaluating the micro-enterprise's financial requirements, managing credit, promoting training, and providing continuing support to production, distribution and marketing; a network of enterprise counsellors; a schedule of 60 micro-enterprises per counsellor per year; a micro-enterprise credit programme; improving the efficiency and institutional capacity of the executing agencies; and training for NGO personnel. The short term goals of the programme for 1988-1990 were to grant loans to 40 000 micro-enterprises, to generate at least 100 000 new jobs, to increase management skills of the 40 000 micro-entrepreneurs, and to democratize credit. Loans to micro-enterprises are channelled through Guatemala's Banco de los Trabajadores. In 1988, the programme financed 3 671 micro-enterprise projects ($4.7 million) and 210 loans to micro-enterprises ($118 000) for participation in the first urban micro-enterprise fair. The average number of jobs created was 2.2 per enterprise for a total of 4 464 jobs. The programme received technical assistance from the UNDP and the Netherlands, and technical co-operation and financial support from the IDB, Belgium, Taiwan, USAID, and the Federal Republic of Germany.

In Brazil, the Rio de Janeiro state industrial development company (CODIN) has been financing, since 1985, a handicrafts promotion scheme called the Programa Produzir, whose central feature is a city showroom in downtown Rio de Janeiro which served as a wholesale marketing window and transactions intermediary for 836 of the 1 935 participating artisans in 1988. The administrative costs, including support of a marketing staff of 20 officials, are fully borne by the state government. The promoters proposed partial privatisation of the activity in 1988, with the participation of an NGO which would charge 15 per cent commission on sales.

In Uruguay, a programme to support wool and cotton textile production by rural artisans, called Manos de Uruguay and based in Montevideo, was established in 1968 grouping 18 production cooperatives with over a thousand participating artisans. Output is marketed through eight shops in Uruguay and to abroad ($4 million per year). Export sales were initially made through ad hoc intermediaries after photos of one of the handmade products of Manos de Uruguay appeared in the French fashion magazine Elle. With technical assistance from the IDB, the organization eventually set up a marketing company in the United States with a US partner. A similar arrangement has been made in Japan. In other countries, Manos de Uruguay markets through local agents.

In Argentina, the Fundación Banco de la Provincia de Córdoba has been responsible since 1983 for an IDB-financed provincial credit and financial intermediation programme for micro-producers and rural growth. The programme had to face the problem of collecting amounts due on loans made to borrowers who cannot provide normal commercial banking guaranties. The solution found was for the programme to purchase the capital goods needed by the borrowing micro-producers and to deliver the goods to them under a rental contract (a variant of a hire-purchase contract). The monthly rental is calculated on the basis of the value of the goods divided by the number of months plus a 4 per cent annual service charge. To cover risks of fire and theft, the programme takes out an insurance contract for the borrower. Non-payment during two consecutive months is grounds for repossessing the capital goods from the borrower with no other legal formalities required. When the loan is fully paid, ownership of the capital good passes to the borrower.

In Chile, the Banco del Desarrollo of Santiago grew out of a savings, loan and industrial credit cooperative set up by a private voluntary organization linked to the Catholic Church of Santiago, the Fundación para el Desarrollo, which then acquired a financial company, the Financiera de Interès Social (FINTESA) which in turn later merged with the Banco Empresarial de Fomento and the Sociedad Financiera Latinamericano de Desarrollo (FLANDES) to form the Banco del Desarrollo. The principal shareholders in the Banco del Desarrollo were the above-mentioned Fundación para el Desarrollo and the federations for small industry and handicrafts, retail commerce, and cooperatives. The bank deals primarily with small and medium scale enterprises (SMEs) rather than micro-enterprises. However, the bank maintains the principle of access by micro-enterprises. One example was a loan to a group of 340 itinerant vendors in Concepción to create and install a marketplace on a piece of land that they had purchased with the results of individual contributions of $0.40 per week during almost three years. To facilitate access, the Banco del Desarrollo has made agreements with NGOs to provide technical assistance to potential borrowers; it also created, together with other national and foreign institutions, a capital fund to finance productive projects of micro-enterprises which are high-risk projects by definition.

C. USAID's PISCES-II Micro-Enterprise Projects

The US Agency for International Development Agency's Programme for Investment in the Small Capital Enterprise Sector (PISCES), funded out of Washington, DC in 1978, was designed to explore the feasibility of direct assistance to micro-enterprises. The first phase of the programme (PISCES-I) examined 20 micro-enterprise projects in 16 countries to identify the elements of their success or failure. The second phase of the programme (PISCES-II)[6] designed, implemented and evaluated four demonstration projects in cooperation with USAID missions in the Dominican Republic, Costa Rica, Kenya, and Egypt. Each of the projects was carried out through a local private voluntary organization (PVO). Technical assistance was provided by ACCION International/AITEC, a consulting group based in Boston, Massachusetts.

The PISCES-II Dominican Republic project was implemented through the Dominican Development Foundation which established an urban micro-enterprise development project (PRODEME) in Santo Domingo in 1981. PRODEME was funded from several sources including the USAID Mission to the Dominican Republic, the Inter-American Foundation, Appropriate Technology International, and local Dominican sources. The project had two components: a mutual loan guaranty component under which small "solidarity groups" of 5 to 8 members guarantied loans for business purposes made to the group; and a micro-enterprise component under which loans and management assistance were extended to individual business owners. In the first 18 months of the project, 343 loans averaging $233 per member were made to solidarity groups with nearly 2 000 members and 211 loans averaging $1 817 were made to individual micro-entrepreneurs. Loans were extended at a flat rate of interest of 24 per cent per year (compared with up to 20 per cent per day charged by money lenders in the informal credit market) and were repayable in 52 weekly installments. The bulk (83 per cent) of the solidarity group clients were itinerant vendors selling their wares from rented tricycle carts; the project lent $249 to each *triciclero* to purchase his tricycle cart and $21 for working capital. The other 17 per cent were seamstresses, food vendors, and market stall vendors who received loans of up to $249 for working capital only. The solidarity group component of the project was slow in issuing loans and ran into serious problems with loan repayment within the first year. The micro-enterprise component dealt with enterprises that already had some capital investment (on average $4 272) and employed an average of 2.2 full-time equivalent workers. The impact of the loans and technical assistance in book-keeping and management was to increase investment, employment (by 1.4 new jobs per enterprise), turnover and net return to the micro-entrepreneur. Pay-back rates were mediocre.

The PISCES-II Costa Rica project for aid to urban businesses was initiated in San Jose in October 1982 and implemented through the Banco Popular y de Desarrollo Comunal, which was already making loans to small industrial enterprises and for low-cost housing. With financing from USAID/Costa Rica for a revolving loan fund, the Banco Popular started extending "solidarity guaranty" loans also to micro-enterprises that were members of solidarity groups. The interest rate charged was 21.5 per cent per year on a declining balance, with repayment in 52 weekly installments. There was no technical assistance component. By October 31, 1983, 83 loans averaging $247 had been granted to solidarity groups totalling 447 members (63 per cent male and 37 per cent female). The categories of loan recipients were the following: street vendors (27 per cent), owners of very small stores such as fruit stands and mini-restaurants (35 per cent), micro-industries and services such as shoemakers and seamstresses (34 per cent), and other businesses (4 per cent). As in the Dominican Republic project, solidarity groups had 8-10 members. The impact of the loans was to create a considerable increase in business activity and income of the recipients and some new employment (0.3 persons per enterprise). Late payment rates were low.

The PISCES-II project in Kenya was implemented through the National Council of Churches of Kenya (NCCK). The NCCK had already in 1975 established a Small Business Scheme, which Fred O'Regan identified for PISCES-I as an appropriate PVO vehicle for channelling assistance to micro-enterprises. The aim of the NCCK's Small Business Scheme was "to help poor, usually illiterate, sometimes disabled, principally female and at times totally inexperienced business operators to increase and then stabilize their incomes and improve the quality of their family life." Although the results of the PISCES-II project were mixed, it demonstrated that "a small-business project, properly designed, can serve the truly poor and that the very poor self-employed can utilize credit and other assistance effectively to improve their standard of living." Under PISCES-II, USAID/Kenya put $275 000 into the NCCK to cover Nairobi, Mombasa, Kisumu/Katanga and Nakuru/Eldoret and to expand the Small Business Scheme revolving fund to a total of $110 000. The project hired and trained a group of urban extension agents to provide business advisory services to the NCCK social workers, to expand project out-reach, to coordinate the delivery and collection of loan funds, and to deliver basic managerial and accounting assistance to individual and group enterprises. In order to integrate the Small Business Scheme into the NCCK's wider Urban Community Improvement Programme, all clients of the Small Business Scheme were interviewed (and in many cases referred) by the NCCK's social workers. Most of the loans were made to provide working capital. Interest on loans was charged by the project at 8 per cent, which was below commercial rates. Fixed collateral requirements were waived. Individual applicants were required to have three third-party cosigners. Groups could guaranty loans collectively. In addition to basic business advice, the project also provided social-work assistance to help resolve personal and family problems underlying many of the business difficulties of the micro-entrepreneurs. Around 75 per cent of the clients of the Small Business Scheme were women. The typical client is "a middle-aged female between 30 and 50 years of age, possessing little or no education, and living in an urban slum area with anywhere from 5 to 14 dependents"; most clients were petty retailers. The Small Business Scheme initially helped generate income for its poor clients and created a number of new job opportunities but monthly profit levels subsequently fell off as business capital was diverted to household use. Loan repayment was a major problem of the project, especially in the bigger cities, Nairobi and Mombasa.

The PISCES-II project in Egypt was an income and employment generation programme initiated in 1980 and implemented through the Coptic Evangelical Organization for Social Services (CEOSS) which serves both Christians and Muslims in the Minya and Assiut provinces of Middle Egypt. USAID/Egypt provided close to 70 per cent of the programme's budget of about $535 000 for the three years 1983-1985. The initial component of the CEOSS programme, a loans-for-development project, started in 1980 with funding from European sources. The CEOSS grant agreement with USAID/Egypt was signed in May 1983 with the US PVO Catholic Relief Services (CRS) as administrative and financial intermediary. Loans varied in size with interest rates set on a case-by-case basis ranging from zero per cent for the poorest clients to 4 per cent or 6 per cent per year for more established clients and second-time borrowers. A second component, loans for community-owned projects, worked through village development committees. A third component, a project for assistance to group enterprises not connected to village development committees, was slow in getting started. CEOSS also established and implemented a skills training programme, initially in sewing (for women) and in woodworking and carpentry, and then in electrical work, plumbing, and house-painting. Given the complexity of the CEOSS programme, loans were made cautiously and progress was slow.

In each of the PISCES-II projects, administration of the credit fund was difficult since small local PVOs have little experience in administering loans, which is the function of a bank or other financial institution rather than of a normal social welfare service organization. The solidarity group innovation helps to improve repayment performance but loan supervision remains a time-consuming and implicitly costly operation.

D. USAID/Senegal's Kaolack Project

The small enterprise (mostly micro-enterprise) component of USAID/Senegal's Community and Enterprise Development project in Kaolack has been in operation since 1986[7]. Results of a 1985 survey showed that access to credit was the major constraint to small businesses development in the region. The strategy adopted was, therefore, to provide a credit service that would respond to the needs of informal sector clients and to keep training and advisory services to a minimum. The approach adopted was to make credit available to people with existing businesses who wish to expand their activities.

The programme has a network of seven store-front field offices in the most important centers of the Kaolack and Fatick regions of Senegal, each manned by a single field officer who is responsible for a geographical zone and for processing loan applications, all of which originate from the field offices. Field officers come from the same milieu as the clients and have modest, but adequate, educational qualifications. They receive intensive field-based training in loan proposal analysis and loan tracking for six months before becoming operational.

An enterprise owner needing a loan to develop his activities first discusses his idea with the field officer. If the field officer judges the idea to have merit, he prepares a loan proposal, which requires detailed planning, including financial analysis, and involves at least one visit to the client's place of business. Once the loan proposal documentation is sent to the head office, a supervisor from the head office and the field officer visit the client at his place of business to discuss the proposal. If the supervisor's appraisal of the proposal and the client is favourable, the proposal is submitted to the loan committee for approval. The time-frame for the approval of an average loan is one month. Loan size and the repayment schedule are calculated in accordance with cash flow of the project to be funded. For first-time loans the maximum loan amount is fixed at CFAF 3 000 000 ($3 000) with a maximum duration of up to 12 months. Second loan amounts and durations are judged according to the needs of the loan project. The interest rate is 22 per cent and is variable according to Central Bank regulations. The primary guarantee is the viability of the loan proposal. The primary loan security is confidence that the project will generate enough revenue to cover its own costs and make enough profit to repay the loan and cover the client's family needs. Clients usually repay their loans on a monthly basis either to the head office cashier, or to their local office. Payments are tracked closely at the head office and late payments are quickly followed up by a visit from a head office programme officer. Late payment situations are also closely tracked by field officers. Loans that are non-performing for more than 90 days are foreclosed with initiation of legal proceedings for seizure of collateral.

During the first two and a half years of the small business programme, of the 384 loans made for a total value of CFAF 486 million ($486 000), 150 loans were fully repaid with interest. The loan default rate was low, and only 15 loans became non-performing, representing a provisional loss of 4.5 per cent of total funds borrowed and paid back to date. The average loan in the outstanding portfolio was CFAF 1.2 million ($1 200 at $1 = CFAF 1 000) for an average duration of 9 months. The main purposes of the loans were working capital (72 per cent), purchase of equipment (13 per cent), and both working capital and equipment (15 per cent).

In the judgment of its managers, the loan programme of the USAID/Senegal's small enterprise project in Kaolack generated the following lessons:

a) Informal sector businesses are viable since many informal sector business people run highly profitable operations by traditional methods. Many of the Kaolack loan programme's clients have a return on capital of more than 100 per cent per year.

b) Informal sector businesses are marginally bankable if appropriate credit analysis techniques are used to evaluate the entrepreneur, his business, and his loan project. It is possible in the short term to recover transaction and default costs from interest and other fees in order to make the lending operation self-sustaining, providing that the loan funds are provided without cost by a donor agency. A larger programme would be needed to generate sufficient loan volume and revenue to pay for capital and to generate a profit. However, the commercial banks in Senegal are not interested in taking over the portfolio of the project because the banks are still unable to collect bad debts from earlier government agricultural campaigns. One of the major banks closed its branch in Kaolack during 1988.

c) Informal sector borrowers do not need to be literate, not do they have to keep written accounts in order to use and repay loans.

d) A "minimalist" approach is effective and economic. It may not be necessary to provide training since the traditional sector has its own vocational training systems and borrowers are capable of making good use of finance without counselling so long as the loan proposal is carefully analyzed, discussed, and agreed upon before it is funded.

e) Modest and accessible storefront offices staffed by field agents without high level qualifications are efficient. The people most likely to succeed as field agents are those who are most like the clients.

f) The interest rate question is controversial. Interest rates in Senegal are governed by the central bank (BCEAO) for all West African CFAF zone countries. The government regards informal businesses as frail and unprofitable and is uneasy about high interest rates on informal sector loans, while the banks claim that under present regulations they cannot lend to small businesses and recover their transaction costs, let alone cover risk. The result of present regulations to protect small businesses from "usurious" rates of interest is that they are completely denied access to credit. The USAID small business programme in Kaolack demonstrated that informal sector businesses are relatively insensitive to interest rates; the programme could probably raise its interest rate to 40 per cent per year without any loss of business or any increase in the default rate.

E. The AID Micro-Enterprise Stock-Taking of 1989

A 1989 evaluation of micro-enterprise projects funded by the US Agency for International Development[8] covered 38 projects or sub-projects in 20 countries of Asia and the Near East, Africa, and Latin America (including the PISCES-II and USAID/Senegal Kaolack projects reviewed in Sections 4.C and 4.D above) initiated in the 1970s and 1980s. Of the 38, 11 were credit projects, 5 were technical assistance and training projects (one with a policy component), and 22 combined credit and technical assistance; 3 were implemented by governments, 3 through government banks, 4 as government projects, 1 through cooperatives, 2 through credit unions, 17 through indigenous private voluntary organizations (PVOs), 2 through affiliated PVOs, and 6 through US PVOs.

The AID evaluation distinguishes between integrative programmes (the enterprise formation approach), minimalist programmes (the enterprise expansion approach), and business development programmes (the enterprise transformation approach). In which group a project is categorized seems to be somewhat arbitrary since the USAID/Senegal Kaolack project managers considered their project to be a minimalist programme (see Section 4.D above) but the AID/Washington evaluation considered it to be a business development programme. One of the important conclusions of the evaluation was that direct assistance programmes that aim to improve the performance of micro-enterprises without attempting to transform them into more complex businesses (the so-called minimalist credit model that provides enterprises with working capital) have a better record of achievement than do the more ambitious transformational programmes. However, the minimalist approach has significant limitations: it is successful because its limited funds usually get applied to the more competent of the pool of potential programme clients. Furthermore, according to the AID evaluation, the needs of the vast majority of micro-enterprises cannot be satisfied merely by provision of small working capital loans. How to reach enterprises whose needs cannot be satisfied by the minimalist strategy is still not clear.

The country information that follows is extracted from the ten country field assessment annexes that form part of the AID/Washington evaluation report.

The largest USAID-funded micro-enterprise project in Bangladesh is the $850 000 village industries oriented Women's Entrepreneurship Development Project, a small project compared to other USAID/Bangladesh activities. The executing agency for the project is the parastatal Bangladesh Small and Cottage Industries Corporation (BSCIC), which provides technical assistance while the Agricultural Bank administers the project's loan component. All project beneficiaries are women. The project identifies actual or potential entrepreneurs and provides skills training, management training, project appraisal services, loan application assistance, and business counselling. Project field staff act as loan collectors on behalf of the Agricultural Bank. Production training can last a month or two; management training typically lasts two or three days. As of the end of 1988, the project had made 10 400 loans, of which 15 per cent were second or third loans. The project had identified 15 560 potential clients and processed 11 700 loan applications, of which 10 530 were approved by the bank. Maximum loan size as of end-1988 was $938. The interest rate was 16 per cent. The loan recovery rate was only 47 per cent in July-September 1988, a sharp fall from its 80 per cent level in the period FY 1985/86 - FY 1986/87. All of the project's expenditures are covered out of the USAID grant and local counterpart; all interest on loans is paid to the Agricultural Bank. The field evaluation found that few of the women producers knew much about the business aspects of the enterprise: in 73 per cent of the businesses, investment decisions were made by the client's husband or father and in 63 per cent, accounts were kept by the husband or father. Project loans were made primarily for food processing (e.g. rice-husking), cottage industry activities (e.g. cane and bamboo basket making, mat-making, tailoring, and net making), and livestock raising and fish farming.

USAID's micro-enterprise programmes in Indonesia are of two types: support of institutions such as the National Cooperative Business Association and local PVOs; and financial support to enterprise development through a Financial Institutions Development project and the Central Java Enterprise Development project. The purpose of the Financial Institutions Development project is to support the development of existing rural credit institutions. The project has two components, a Village Finance Institutions sub-project modelled after a relatively unsubsidized and growing financial institution, Central Java's Badan Kredit Kecamatan (BKK); and KUPEDES, the General Village Credit programme of the Bank Rakyat Indonesia. The Village Finance Institutions sub-project provides start-up funding, training and technical assistance to regional development banks and incorporates financial institutions established at the sub-district (*kecamatan*) or village levels. The KUPEDES sub-project provides technical assistance and training. Loans issued by institutions participating in the Village Finance Institutions sub-project range from a minimum of Rp. 5 000 ($11) to a maximum of Rp. 500 000 ($1 111), for a normal 12-week term with no collateral other than endorsement of the village chief and at an interest rate of 10 per cent on the 12 week loan amount disbursed (*i.e.*, an annual rate of 43 per cent although late payments reduce the effective rate to 20 or 30 per cent). Loans issued under KUPEDES range from Rp. 25 000 ($55) to Rp. 3.0 million ($6 666), for a 12-month term for working capital loans and 36 months for investment loans, with land or property as collateral and at an interest rate of 1.5 per cent per month on the original amount for investment loans and 2 per cent per month for working capital loans. Working capital loans accounted for 96 per cent of the KUPEDES portfolio in January 1988, when the average size of loan was Rp. 535 000 ($326). Most of the resources of KUPEDES come from Government of Indonesia grants and savings deposits.

Among the institutions receiving USAID support are: a) the Puskowanjati Women's Cooperative umbrella organization in East Java to which USAID has provided grants totalling $505 000 since 1984 for the establishment or expansion of revolving loan funds for member cooperatives and for training in management and financing administration; and b) the Maha Bhoga Marga micro-enterprise development programme in Bali to which USAID made a grant of $180 000 in 1987, of which $88 400 was set aside as a contribution to a revolving loan fund.

In Egypt, USAID set up two funds for loans to micro-enterprises. One was the Coptic Evangelical Organization for Social Services (CEOSS) PISCES-II sub-project, discussed in Section 4.C above, to which USAID/Egypt made a grant of $314 800 in local currency counterpart funds in 1983 of which $312 000 had been expended by CEOSS through August 1986 and the remainder refunded to USAID. The other was the Small Enterprise Loan programme to which $180 000 was granted in 1982 out of the multi-million dollar Helwan Housing Project to set up a revolving credit fund; the Government of Egypt contributed a matching amount to the revolving fund. The purpose of the Small Enterprise Loan programme was to expand or improve established micro-enterprises in seven squatter communities in Helwan, and to make loans to residents to open new businesses. The Helwan revolving fund has been fully loaned out since 1985. Between 1982 and 1988, some 317 loans were made; average size of loan in 1988 was $780. Loans were issued for 20 months at 10 per cent interest plus 3 per cent in origination and collection fees, which represents a negative real rate of interest. The loan fund is being sharply eroded by inflation (22 per cent in 1988).

In Cameroun, the USAID activity most directly related to micro-enterprises is a $4.8 million grant to the Cameroun Cooperative Credit Union League (CamCCUL) through the World Council of Credit Unions (WOCCU). The CamCCUL is mainly an anglophone movement, but with affiliates in five provinces. In June 1988, it had 68 460 members, 121 registered credit unions and 114 discussion groups, total savings (shares) of $31.2 million and total loans outstanding of $21.5 million. Some 70 per cent of a 1987 sample of $6.1 million of CamCCUL loans were made for construction, education and health purposes; only 19 per cent were made for business purposes (15 per cent for trade and 4 per cent for farming). Despite the size of credit union assets and loans, Cameroun lacks credit union legislation.

In Malawi, the US is currently providing financial support to the Development of Malawi Traders Trust (DEMATT) ($760 000) and the Malawi Union of Savings and Credit Cooperatives (MUSCCO) ($1.4 million) as part of a $5.8 million USAID Rural Enterprise and Agribusiness Development Institutions project grant. In 1986/87 DEMATT provided business and technical advisory services to 545 enterprises in trade (37 per cent), production (54 per cent), and services (9 per cent). MUSCCO is a credit union movement whose aims are to stimulate savings and to facilitate group-based lending, mostly to agriculture but to a limited extent also to small shopkeepers and artisans.

In Senegal, USAID is providing support to micro-enterprises through the Community and Enterprise Development project in Kaolack discussed in Section 4.D above. USAID/Senegal proposes extending the project to the Thiès region and possibly to initiate and to fund a similar project in suburban Dakar.

In the Dominican Republic, USAID is currently supporting micro-enterprises (in 1988, $2.2 million) through two intermediary institutions. The first is the Asociación para del Desarrollo de Microempresas Inc. (ADEMI) which provides credit and occasional technical assistance to micro-enterprises in Santo Domingo and throughout the country. The ADEMI project emerged from the PISCES-II Programa de Desarrollo de Microempresas (PRODEME) discussed in Section 4.C above. ADEMI defines micro-enterprises as businesses in operation at least a year with six or fewer employees and less than $1 600 in fixed assets. Loan amounts and terms are increased for repeat borrowers. The average size of enterprises obtaining an initial loan is $1 000 in assets and three employees. The second intermediary institution is the Programa de Asistencia a la Pequeña Empresa (PROAPE) which provides managerial training and conducts feasibility studies for micro-enterprises and passes them on to the Fondo para el Desarrollo (FONDESA) for financing. PROAPE and FONDESA are separate divisions within the Asociación para el Desarrollo Inc. (APEDI) in Santiago, the Dominican Republic's second largest city. Requests for larger loans are passed on to the Small Industry Development Programme of the Fondo de Inversiones para el Desarrollo Economico (FIDE) which also receives USAID support. The PROAPE/FONDESA micro-enterprise programme focuses on businesses with sales of less than $12 000 per year, net worth of less than $7 200, and investment per job of no more than $1 433 (while the small enterprise programme targets slightly larger enterprises). PROAPE also deals with solidarity groups consisting usually of five members in similar activities. As of October 1988, PROAPE/FONDESA had made loans to 583 small and micro-enterprises (average size of initial loan $796), and it had assisted 332 solidarity groups with 1 641 members (average size of initial loan $398).

In Ecuador, a three-year $4.5 million USAID project, approved on July 30, 1986, provided for credit, technical assistance and representational services to small enterprises, but the representational component was not implemented as of 1989. The credit component is being administered by CARE (which took over from Partnership for Productivity in 1987) with ACCION and the Fundación Caraval as subcontractors. ACCION is providing technical assistance to micro-enterprises through two existing programmes, in Guayaquil through the Fundación Eugenio Espejo (FEE) and in Quito through the Fundación Ecuatoriana de Desarrollo (FED), which target micro-entrepreneurs with fewer than five employees and solidarity groups of street vendors. USAID did not provide any direct funding for loans under the ACCION component. However, funding was obtained from the Inter-American Development Bank for small loans at 5 per cent interest per month. Over half of the loan beneficiaries have been women. The Fundación Carvajal is implementing technical assistance to micro-entrepreneurs (who pay user fees) in five coastal cities of Ecuador under the credit component of the project. A credit fund for the coastal city micro-entrepreneurs was financed with $200 000 of local currency counterpart of US assistance using the Corporación Financiera Nacional as the intermediary to local banks. CARE itself is providing assistance to the Fondo de la Pequeña Industria y Artesenia (FOPINAR) set up within the Corporación Financiera Nacional and to provincial Credit Guaranty Corporations and the Retroguaranty Fund to strengthen existing credit and credit guaranty mechanisms to "graduate" micro-enterprises from special micro-enterprise credit programmes to the commercial portfolio of private financial institutions. FOPINAR has received funding from the World Bank and the Netherlands.

The technical assistance component of USAID/Ecuador's Small Enterprise Development project is being implemented by the Institute of Socioeconomic and Technical Research (INSOTEC), which provides industry-specific technical assistance to labour-intensive micro-enterprises that use local materials and have linkages to other domestic industries. The target is to reach 500 small enterprises. USAID and INSOTEC signed a grant agreement on September 30, 1988 to form a credit fund of $600 000 for loans to beneficiaries of the INSOTEC training and technical assistance programmes.

USAID/Ecuador is also supporting a skills training programme for micro-enterprises through a three-year grant of $596 000 and $227 000 of local currency counterpart funds to the Instituto de Capacitación para la Pequeña Empresa Industrial (INCAPI).

In Guatemala, USAID financed a variety of projects with small and micro-scale enterprise components in the 1980s, among them: a) a women-in-development project in support of the Fundación para el Desarrollo de la Mujer (FDM) which provides credit, training and limited technical assistance to micro-enterprises owned by groups of two or more women, through a PVO umbrella organization; b) a rural enterprise project that provides support to the Corporación Financiera Nacional (CORFINA) for financing of rural enterprises and to the Instituto Tecnico de Capacitación (INTECAP) for technical assistance and appropriate technology research; c) a cooperative development project that provides support to the National Credit Union Federation of Guatemala; d) a micro-business promotion project that provides support to the Fundación de Asistencia para la Pequeña Empresa (FAPE) as part of a programme under the Office of the Vice-President called the Sistema Multiplicador de la Micro-Empresa (SIMME), cited in section 4.B above. The Inter-American Development Bank (IDB) and the UNDP also have been contributing to SIMME and to related PVO programmes.

In Paraguay, the small USAID programme contributes some support to the Fundación Paraguaya de Cooperación y Desarrollo which provides training, credit, technical assistance and loan supervision to micro-commerce (street vendors, market women, and small retailers), and micro-producers of goods (shoes, leather products, clothing, metal articles) and services (electrical, mechanical and metal goods repair). The Fundación has also received financing from the Small Projects programme of the IDB. The Fundación charges 6 per cent interest per month on the full amount of the principal for the whole period loan, equal to an annual rate of interest of 132 per cent. Local moneylenders charge as much as 20 per cent per day. Delinquency rates on Fundación loans are around 10 per cent.

F. The ILO Informal Sector Support Project for Francophone Africa

The ILO/Swiss Cooperation research project on training for the informal sector in francophone Africa initiated by Georges Nihan in the 1970s was followed up in the 1980s under the supervision of Carlos Maldonado by an informal sector action programme, financed by the UNDP and the Swiss Fund for Technical Cooperation and implemented in three of the countries where studies had been carried out: Mali, Rwanda and Togo[9]. The central aim of the programme is to encourage small-scale urban producers to organize themselves to get greater control over the business decisions that affect their lives rather than to be dependent upon the decisions of outsiders. Accordingly, the programme seeks to organize producer groups on a durable basis rather than aiming at immediate material benefits. As originally proposed by Nihan, one of the instruments introduced in each city is a central workshop to allow artisans easier access to basic equipment and infrastructure. The programme has also had training and credit components. The target groups have in practice been small and micro scale entrepreneurs (and their employees and apprentices) in a variety of occupations:

carpenters, blacksmiths, masons, electricians, plumbers, painters, vehicle and other repairmen, and other crafts. In Mali, the programme has also provided special support to unemployed youths and women to enable them to establish businesses on their own.

The programme's organizational efforts were particularly effective in Rwanda where artisans in Kigali got together to negotiate with the local authorities to be issued work cards granting them resident rights in the city and thereby exemption from police raids. The artisans were then able to negotiate the granting of bank loans (after establishment of a mutual savings scheme), reductions in local taxes, and the right to occupy public land. Grassroots associations have been set up in Kigali and in three other towns in Rwanda. In Mali, associations have been set up in Bamako and in four other towns. In Togo, the ILO programme has worked with an artisans' association, the Groupement Interprofessionel des Artisans du Togo (GIPATO) in Lomé and in Sokodé. The programme has been more successful in Sokodé where the artisans are organized by trade (*métier*) than in Lomé where the project is organized by neighbourhood (*quartier*)[10].

The workshops in Togo and Mali have served as sources of equipment to micro-producers on a rental basis and as locales for training masters and apprentices. The workshops also keep stocks of raw materials and provide space for the display and sale of goods produced by the artisans.

The artisans' associations involved in the ILO programme have been able to mobilize savings of their members on a group basis in order to get access to bank credit. In Rwanda, the collective savings of the confederation of artisans' associations are blocked to constitute a guaranty for loans issued to groups of savers by the People's Banks (*Banques Populaires*). In 1986, the Kigali artisans' confederation negotiated the establishment of a separate bank linked to the People's Banks; its capital is constituted by savings of the artisans and its board of directors consists of seven artisans. In Togo, the Sokodé GIPATO established a mutual savings and loan fund which is functioning.

The training component of the ILO programme has been implemented as an adjunct to traditional methods of skill transmission through experienced local artisans. In Bamako and in Togo, the programme's training activities were directed first at apprentices (technical training in carpentry, blacksmithing, and construction work) and then at the artisans themselves (management training in cost-estimating, book-keeping, new products, and literacy). In Kigali, training activities focused on enterprise management, technical training (in iron working, welding, electro-mechanics and shoemaking), and literacy.

One of the difficulties run into by the ILO programme and related programmes such as the Projet Germano-Togolais pour la Promotion de l'Artisanat in Lomé has been the tendency of the older and best-off artisans to take over the associations for their own benefit and to try to freeze out the younger and less well-off members. The associations have, nevertheless, demonstrated that grass-roots initiatives and mobilization of local resources can be effective in promoting micro-enterprise activity.

G. Small Enterprise Projects Supported by the World Bank and Other Donor Agencies

In addition to the ILO, the Inter-American Development Bank and the US Agency for International Development whose programmes have been discussed above, other multilateral and bilateral aid agencies are also providing support to small (and micro) scale enterprises in the developing countries, among them the World Bank, UNIDO, NORAD, RVB Netherlands, UNDP, the UN Capital Development Fund, the Asian Development Bank, the European

Investment Bank, the EEC's European Development Fund, and the aid agencies of the F.R. of Germany.   Jacob Levitsky's 1989 paper for NORAD on the effectiveness of donor agency support for small enterprise development provides a succint review of a number of such projects[11].

The World Bank approved 70 different projects in 36 countries between 1973 and 1988 for a total of over \$3 billion for on-lending by local financial intermediaries to small scale enterprises.   Only in Nepal, Sri Lanka and Indonesia did the loans go to very small units, micro-enterprises and cottage industries with an average size of loan of less than \$5 000.   In most World Bank projects in Asia and Latin America, average size of loan was between \$20 000 and \$60 000, an indication that the loan recipients were small-scale rather than micro-scale, although in some middle-income countries such as Korea, Colombia and Mexico, a significant portion of the loans went to medium-scale enterprises.   In projects using mainly commercial banks as intermediaries, loan repayment rates were high, particularly in Latin America (Mexico, Peru, Ecuador) but less so in Asia.   Where projects used development finance institutions as intermediaries, some achieved high recovery rates but they were generally less successful.   More recently the World Bank has been active in developing projects focused directly on micro-enterprises as part of its concern with the social dimensions of adjustment.

The African Development Bank, the European Investment Bank, and the European Development Fund have made loans for small scale enterprise development in Africa, usually using the same intermediaries as do World Bank projects.   The UN Capital Development fund has used its limited resources both for direct lending to small scale enterprises and as guaranties and quasi-equity.

Among the bilateral agencies, the West German KFW and the Netherlands FMO have provided limited financing for loans to small scale enterprises in Africa, Latin America, and Asia.   AID/Washington's Private Sector Revolving Fund has been issuing loans and loan guarantees for on-lending to small scale enterprises since 1983.

In Bangladesh, the World Bank and other donors have become frustrated with the parapublic Bangladesh Small and Cottage Industry Corporation (BSCIC) which was the major financial intermediary for loans to small scale enterprises from the 1960s; instead the donors have been placing increasing reliance on NGOs, the best known of which is the Grameen Bank which, as a bank for the poor, made over 400 000 loans between 1983 and 1988 at an average size of \$60 each.   The Grameen Bank has received funding from IFAD, SIDA, NORAD and the Ford Foundation.   The rural-oriented Micro-Industries Development Association Society (MIDAS) is receiving aid from USAID, NORAD, Switzerland, the Ford Foundation, and UNIDO.   However, with an average size of loan of \$80 000, MIDAS appears to be operating more as a small industry development bank than as a micro-enterprise development agency.   There were at least 10 more major NGOs assisting small cottage industries and micro-enterprises in Bangladesh in 1990.

In Indonesia, the KIK/KMKP scheme, started in 1973 with assistance from the Netherlands, provided credit on a large scale to very small indigenous Indonesian enterprises. By 1988, the KIK/KMKP programme had provided loans for investment (through KIK) and for working capital (through KMKP) to around 2.5 million borrowers for a total value of over \$2.5 billion.   The World Bank made its first loan to the KIK/KMKP programme in 1978. Most of the programme's resources have been provided by the Government of Indonesia. The programme was implemented mostly through state and regional banks.   Unfortunately, loan recovery rates were low and the World Bank made no further loans to the programme after 1986. Technical assistance to small enterprises in Indonesia has been provided mainly by bilateral donors (F.R. of Germany, Netherlands, Australia) as well as the EEC and UNIDO. Over a hundred technological institutes in fields such as metals, leather, ceramics and handicrafts have been set up with donor assistance, and over 200 NGOs are operating throughout the country. Two major programmes support rural micro-enterprises: the BKK, a village credit institution operating in Central Java since 1972 which issues loans (average size about $60) with a low level of default and at an interest rate high enough to cover the costs of the programme; and KUPEDES, a rural savings and loan programme initiated in 1984 which has received technical assistance from USAID and in 1987 a $100 million loan from the World Bank.

In Kenya, the major recipient of assistance from the donor community (GTZ and KFW of the F.R. of Germany, SIDA, NORAD, DANIDA, World Bank, EEC, ILO, UNIDO, India and Japan) for small enterprise development has been Kenya Industrial Estates (KIE). Japanese technical assistance has been provided to the Kenya Industrial Training Institute (KITI) in Nakuru since the 1960s. The Netherlands and Germany's Friedrich Ebert Foundation provided funding to create the Small Enterprise Finance Corporation (SEFCO) in 1984. USAID established its Rural Private Enterprise Project in 1984 and has been moving funds, slowly, through the Kenya Commercial Finance Company (KCFC), Barclay's Bank and Standard Bank. Most of the assistance has gone to small and medium scale enterprises with some to large enterprises. USAID has also been channelling funds to the informal sector through local NGOs such as the National Council of Churches of Kenya (NCCK), the Undugu Society, CARE, the Kenya Women Finance Trust, Technoserve, and others (see Section 4.C above).

In Tanzania, assistance from the donor community (SIDA, Germany, UNDP, UNIDO, India, the Netherlands, and Japan) to small scale enterprises since the mid-1970s has been channelled through the Small Industry Development Organization (SIDO). SIDO developed a multifarious programme (20 regional small industry promotion offices, 12 training-and-production centers, over a dozen industrial estates, and a hire purchase programme) which turned out to be too complicated for it to manage.

Zambia established a Village Industry Services (VIS) programme in 1978 with support from NORAD, Italy and Belgium, and a relatively ineffectual Small Industries Development Organization (SIDO) in 1981, patterned after Tanzania's, with assistance from UNIDO. A small enterprise development lending institution, Small-Scale Enterprise Promotion (SEP) Ltd., was established in 1983 with 24.5 per cent of its shares owned by the Friedrich Ebert Foundation of Germany, 24.5 per cent by the Netherlands FMO and the rest by Zambian banks. NORAD has been providing assistance to a Special Fund for Rural Development to guaranty loans to enterprises established more than 50 kms from the central Zambian railway line.

In Peru, the major vocational training institution, Servicio Nacional de Adiestramiento en Trabajo Industial (SENATI), has moved into the provision of assistance to small enterprise with donor support from the UNDP, the ILO, the Netherlands, and the F.R. of Germany. The Germans also helped to create a small industry loan guaranty fund, Fondo de Garantia para la Pequeña Industria (FOGAPI). USAID has been supporting a Rural Development Fund since 1975. The World Bank issued a 1981 loan to finance small scale and artisanal enterprises through a small industry credit programme unit set up inside the Corporación Financiera de Desarrollo (COFIDE) and thence through a network of participating financial intermediaries. The World Bank loan did reach very small enterprises and more than 50 per cent went to borrowers outside the Lima area. USAID and UNIDO have supported industrial estates in Trujillo and in a suburb of Lima. Recently, the Netherlands FMO has provided assistance to micro-enterprises through the Central de Credito Cooperativo (CCC). The IDB and USAID have provided funds for loans to micro-enterprises through local NGOs, among them INDESI and Acción Comunitaria.

H. Informal Sector Programmes: Summary Evaluation

The first programmes in support of small and micro-scale enterprises under the label of promotion of the informal sector were specified in Colombia's national plans early in the 1970s. Since then, micro-enterprise support programmes have mushroomed elsewhere in Latin America as well as in Africa and Asia, encouraged by injections of financial assistance from the bilateral and multilateral aid donor agencies. The main instrument of intervention has been credit, supplemented by technical assistance in production methods, management and marketing, and by some infrastructure.

A significant constraint on formal sector credit to micro-enterprises has been the existence of interest rate ceilings in a number of countries more concerned with the immorality of usury than with the positive contributions of productive efficiency. The same constraint seems to decapitalize the revolving funds that have been set up with donor or national government financing as intermediaries to issue loans to small and micro-scale enterprises. The constraint is not binding where donors have been ready to replenish the revolving funds; but it prevents the development of self-supporting financial intermediaries whose vocation is credit to small and micro-scale enterprises, and it limits the scale of the activity.

Experience with the considerable number of micro-enterprise support programmes discussed in this chapter has shown that "minimalist" credit programmes, those with little or no training or technical assistance added to the credit component, have been successful in increasing the incomes of their borrowers and in maintaining respectably high repayment rates. Such success may be due partly to the fact that funds are limited so that the credit is rationed to the more competent potential borrowers by the process of selecting among candidates for loans. An exception would appear to be the Grameen Bank of Bangladesh, whose loans are extremely small and whose borrowers extremely numerous. It is still not clear how to meet the needs of less viable enterprises on a cost-effective basis.

Notes and References

1. LIEDHOLM and MEAD (1987).
2. KILBY (1979), and KILBY and D'ZMURA (1985).
3. ILO (1970).
4. KUGLER (1982).
5. INTER-AMERICAN DEVELOPMENT BANK (1989).
6. ASHE (1985). The Program for Investment in the Small Capital Enterprise Sector (PISCES) was the first of the zodiac-labelled programmes (PISCES, ARIES and GEMINI) conceived and supervised by Michael Farbman, Chief of the Employment and Enterprise Division of AID/Washington's Bureau for Science and Technology.
7. McKENZIE (1989). See also the final reports on the 1989 USAID Abidjan and Nairobi conferences on The Informal Sector: Issues in Policy Reform and Programs, edited by Deborah M. Orsini for Labat-Anderson Incorporated and AID
8. US AGENCY FOR INTERNATIONAL DEVELOPMENT (1989). The evaluation team also issued separate Micro-Enterprise Stock Taking field assessments for Bangladesh, Indonesia, and Egypt (in AID's Asia and the Near East area), Cameroun, Malawi, and Senegal (in Africa), and the Dominican Republic, Ecuador, Guatemala, and Paraguay (in Latin America).
9. MALDONADO (1989).
10. LUBELL (1989).
11. LEVITSKY (1989).

Chapter 5

SPECIAL ASPECTS OF INFORMALITY

As described in the chapters above, most of the concern of international agencies, national governments, and PVOs with informal sector entities has been focused on macroeconomic policies and on practical programmes to support the more viable of the informal sector's micro-enterprises by extending them credit through special credit institutions or through the banking system, with some supplementary management training and technical assistance provided through governmental agencies and local PVOs. There has, however, also grown up a considerable body of research on special aspects of informality, of which the following are touched upon in the present chapter: street traders; informal housing; women in the informal sector; informal financial markets; technology for the informal sector; training for the informal sector; and the relationship between regulation and informality.

A. Street Traders

Street trading is one of the more intractable informal sector problems faced by municipal authorities of the Third World. The censuses of informal sector activity cited in Chapter 2 above invariably found that the majority of informal sector participants were in commerce - as petty traders in the market places and on the streets of the Third World cities under review. Indeed, street traders are a feature of urban life throughout the world, developed and developing. However, in most of the industrialised countries, street trading is controlled, licensed, and organized in periodic street fairs and permanent flea markets, although with some evident exceptions such as the expatriate Senegalese peddlers on the streets of First World cities from Aix-les-Bains to New York. In Third World cities, where poverty, rural to urban migration, and unemployment are severe, the pressure of street traders on urban space is seen as a universal problem by municipal authorities charged with keeping their cities clean and orderly. The street traders are seen to occupy urban space in a disorderly fashion, to cause traffic congestion, to compete "unfairly" with more formal retail shops, and to be liberally sprinkled with pickpockets and other riffraff. The struggle between the street traders and the authorities is unending; and the authorities usually lose out, but at great cost to the street traders. Repression is sporadic but the threat of repression is constant. Typical is the September 1989 announcement by the President of Mali of an organized police effort to remove street-side vendors and stands cluttering public areas in Bamako[1].

Street trading is one of the points of entry for migrants into the working life of the city, but it is also a traditional life-time activity for many of the working poor. In many cities of Africa and in southeast Asia, street trading, often as seller of prepared food, is one of the major occupations of the urban informal sector's working women. In Togo, particularly along the coast, to be a petty trader operating in the market place or on the street in front of the family dwelling or out of the dwelling itself seems to be almost a reflex of younger and older women to economic precariousness.

The mobile petty trader is in the street because that is where the largest number of potential customers are to be found. The street traders time their presence to the ebb and flow of pedestrian and vehicular traffic, and to the daily cycle of buyer habits. Sellers of prepared foods appear close to office buildings at lunch time and near places of entertainment at night. Fresh food sellers congregate outside organized market places and formal sector supermarkets when housewives and others are provisioning themselves. Non-food sellers hawk their wares when people are on the streets but not necessarily intent on getting something to eat. The conflict with the authorities arises when the street traders invade the modern town centre and give it a disorderly appearance, or worse, cause traffic congestion. The municipal authorities are also concerned with the hazards to health and hygiene caused by food sellers. On the other hand, the authorities are aware that the street sellers fill an important function in providing goods and services at relatively low prices to lower income city dwellers, and that they are a source of revenue for the municipal government. Furthermore, there is often a symbiotic relationship between street traders and established formal sector enterprises that leads to ambiguity as to the "independent" status of some of the street traders[2].

Examples of the situation of street traders in Lima (Peru) and in Santiago (Chile) have been discussed in Chapter 2. The classic studies on hawkers in southeast Asia carried out by Terence McGee and his colleagues[3] saw the tensions between the street traders and the authorities as a reflection of the conflict between the spatial needs of modern technology (particularly the automobile) as perceived by the authorities, and the persistence of traditional modes of city living, especially in the Chinese cultural areas of southeast Asia. The McGee studies dealt with the two city-states, Hong Kong and Singapore, and with two cities each in Indonesia (Jakarta and Bandung), Malaysia (Kuala Lumpur and Malacca), and the Philippines (Manila and Baguio). The conflict of technologies take several forms that impinge on the activities of street traders. Freeway systems for motor vehicles cut through residential areas, blocking normal pathways for pedestrian customers of the hawkers and the hawkers themselves. Office buildings expand into residential areas and displace the hawkers' low-income customers out of the city's inner core forcing hawkers to become more mobile in order to service increasing population densities on the periphery; in Singapore a system of travelling night-time markets emerged in consequence.

Government attitudes are still basically hostile toward street traders except in Malaysia where the authorities have been encouraging street trading as a means of promoting the economic integration of ethnic Malays into cities dominated by ethnic Chinese. Singapore's attitudes are flexible: the authorities have accompanied public housing programmes and urban renewal schemes with the creation of hawker centres in new housing estates, efforts to move hawkers into public markets, and the refusal to issue new hawker licenses to persons under 40 years of age. Hong Kong, which has to deal with an unending inflow of immigrants, has invested large resources in a Hawker Control Force that fails either to control hawker activities or to reduce the number of hawkers. In Manila, restrictions on hawkers are enforced only in the better-off parts of town. Jakarta puts resources into unsuccessful clearance operations but has also established hawker emporiums (whose rents are too high for most street traders).

McGee identifies three kinds of positive government actions that can diminish the tension between hawkers and the authorities: a) licensing of hawker operations; b) expanding the amount of urban space available to hawkers by expanding public (or private) markets (although off-street locations may be second-best for the hawkers), using open space imaginatively (e.g. converting car parking lots and playgrounds to night-time markets), closing some streets to vehicular traffic and permitting entry of hawkers, and assigning hawkers to secondary streets where they do not block through traffic on main thoroughfares; and c) creating credit institutions for small businessmen including hawkers and subsidizing the creation of market space. McGee describes street trading as both a residual occupation with marginal and submarginal incomes, and an economic ladder that offers some hope of upward mobility.

It is safe to predict that street trading will continue to draw entrants so long as other sources of urban employment lag behind population and labour force increases, and that governments will continue to be faced with the tensions arising from the necessity to combine control and accommodation.

B. Informal Housing

Probably the most widespread informal sector activity since the mass movement of rural to urban migrants throughout the Third World since World War II has been the creation of informal housing, sometimes legal but mostly squatter-built: the *gecekundolar* of Turkey's cities, the *invasiones* of Hispanic Latin America, the *favelas* of Rio de Janeiro, the *bidonvilles* of North Africa, the *bustees* of Calcutta. The history of squatter settlements and of government and international agency efforts to deal with them is well documented and will not be gone into here. It should nevertheless be mentioned that the World Bank invented its sites-and-services projects to help cope with the problem. Concerned governments (such as that of Colombia) devoted resources to legalizing urban land invasions and to training construction workers for self-employment in meeting squatter needs for housing from the late 1960s. Hernando de Soto's description of the irresistible growth of informal settlements in Lima (Peru) and the adjustment of the formal sector and the legal system to the new realities thus created is one of the more fascinating parts of his book on *The Other Path*[4].

The competition between the informal and formal sectors for urban space is even more intense in the field of shelter than it is in street-trading, but the settlements can and do spill outward, extending the built up surface of the cities and creating pressure on municipal governments to provide urban services in the periphery and on informal sector operators to provide transport connecting the new settlements to the urban centre. The demand for informal housing is insatiable: it is partly monetized, employing informal sector building contractors, masons, carpenters, labourers and durable materials, and partly satisfied in kind by self-built housing constructed out of light and/or more durable scavenged or purchased building materials. The economic contribution of informal sector housing is enormous, its contribution to human welfare incalculable.

C. Women in the Urban Informal Sector

Household incomes of the poor urban families are often derived from three sources: earnings in formal sector employment, income from informal sector activity, and subsistence production such as vegetable gardening, the raising of chickens, and repair and construction of housing. In socially fluid urban situations with large seasonal and temporary migration,

Jakarta being a typical example[5], a household member working in the formal sector will provide a steady source of cash income which is supplemented by earnings of other household members (often women) working in informal sector activities and in subsistence production. The proportions vary widely from household to household.

Most working women in the cities of the Third World work in informal sector occupations as petty retail traders, as market women, as prepared-food sellers, or as family workers in household-based enterprises. A few of the market women are well off (e.g., the Mama's Benz of coastal West Africa); but the majority are on the border-line of survival, supplementing family income if they are part of a married household and providing family income when they are unmarried, divorced or widowed heads of household. In most countries they suffer a host of handicaps: the burdens of child-bearing and child-rearing, sex-discriminatory legal disadvantages, social disadvantages that include inferior education or complete lack of access to formal education, lack of access to resources and skills, and the cumulation of income-earning and unpaid household tasks. Growing awareness of the problems of urban women has led to the initiation by governments and NGOs of many small pilot projects to support economic activity by women. An excellent review of the issues and of some project experience was recently published in a Ford Foundation supported special issue of *World Development* (Vol. 17, No. 7, July 1989) on expanding income-earning opportunities for women in developing countries[6]. The discussion here touches on three themes: access to credit, empowerment, and street food trading, the first two of which were developed at length in the *World Development* collection of articles, and the third in the USAID street foods project implemented by Irene Tinker and the Equity Policy Center (EPOC) of Washington, D.C.[7].

Informal sector participants are generally disadvantaged by lack of access to business credit; the situation of women operators is often even worse, although the disadvantage is partly offset by the development of indigenous revolving savings and credit associations established mostly by women for women such as the tontines of West Africa. Among the particular constraints on access by women to credit are non-interest transaction costs such as the transport time required to reach potential lenders, collateral requirements where ownership is legally vested in male household members but not in females, and a variety of cultural factors[8]. A number of NGO credit projects have been established that are specially or largely oriented toward female informal sector participants. Among those frequently cited as having some success in urban areas are the Self-Employed Women's Association (SEWA) of Ahmedabad (India) and the Working Women's Forum (WWF) of Madras[9], and in rural areas the Grameen Bank of Bangladesh and the Bangladesh Rural Advancement Committee (BRAC). An issue that continues to be debated is whether minimalist credit-only programmes are sufficient or whether they should be expanded to include other kinds of support such as marketing assistance, and provision of advice on production and management techniques. Limiting the approach to provision of credit, particularly to a solidarity group, has the advantages of providing a clear indicator of performance (loan repayment rates) and of shifting much of the cost of processing loans from the lending institution to the borrowing group.

The notion of empowerment to offset the double disadvantage of being both poor and female entails reshaping the legal environment and implies the organization of associations of women traders and producers to act as pressure groups. The process of empowerment requires allies among the existing elite, at least at the start. For example, SEWA was originally concerned primarily with the delivery of credit in Ahmadabad but then negotiated to end policy harassment of its informal sector women clients. Direct but non-violent methods of protest, such as the "mooning" of the Marxist-Leninist military rulers of Benin by the market women of Cotonou, can also be effective.

Informal prepared food sellers are another ubiquitous phenomenon of Third World informality with a large female component. Of the four EPOC street foods project case studies mentioned above, the highest rate of women's participation was in Iloilo (Philippines) (90 per cent), followed by Ziguinchor (Senegal) (53 per cent), Bogor (Indonesia) (40 per cent), and Manikganj (Bangladesh) (37 per cent). In Ziguinchor, men and women vendors sold different products, sometimes determined by the capital requirements for operation: men sold hard cookies (called *bonbons*) baked from wheat flour whose production required an oven; yoghurt produced by women was made from whole milk delivered by Peulh herders while yoghurt produced by men was made from powdered milk whose acquisition required a bit of working capital[10]. Women specialized in precooked foods prepared at home while men sold meat-and-onion *brochettes* and herb tea or coffee prepared on the spot. Except in Ziguinchor, the street food traders were subjected to police harassment and forcible removal from the street. Institutional mechanisms are needed to legitimize the presence of the street food traders. The EPOC study recommends the establishment of separate women's vendor groups (partly as an element of empowerment) because it was found that women in mixed groups usually avoid taking active leadership roles.

D. Informal Financial Markets[11]

Most informal sector operators do not participate in or have access to formal financial institutions such as banks, postal savings networks, provident funds, and insurance companies. When they need credit, they borrow from family and friends or from that primary informal financial intermediary, the traditional money lender, or else they obtain short-term supplier credit from traders. Informal credit transactions are carried out on the basis of face-to-face relationships between creditor and debtor. Interest rates are high, but loans are available quickly, and repayment is encouraged by mutual confidence and social pressure (combined with a residual threat of violence in the event of non-payment). In rural areas especially, the moneylender may cumulate economic roles (landlord, produce dealer) that provide other levers for guarantying repayment[12].

Another widespread informal financial institution, about which more and more is being discovered, is the informal mutual saving association of which the tontine is one example. The mutual saving association can take several forms. One is the rotating saving association whose participants agree to make regular contributions to a fund which is placed at the disposition of each contributor in rotation; the fund may or may not make loans to members. Another is the non-rotating saving association whose participants save regularly on a contractual basis; the savings may be used to make loans to members or non-members on either an interest-bearing or an interest-free basis. Straightforward credit associations or money-lending groups lend exclusively to non-members; interest earnings are distributed proportionately to members' contributions.

The country in Africa where informal savings associations and informal saving and credit associations appear to be the most widespread is Cameroun where it is estimated that about 70 per cent of the adult population participates in such informal financial associations, and that total national savings kept by informal financial groups may have been equivalent to 1.2 times the magnitude of all deposits in Cameroun's commercial banks and development banks in March 1988, or 54 per cent of total savings in Cameroun[13]. Some of the individual associations obtain loans from quasi-formal financial institutions such as the national public-sector rural development foundation, a credit union, and an umbrella organization of informal financial associations.

In Senegal and Zaire, whose formal financial systems are in crisis, informal saving arrangements are of considerable importance[14]. Cash is cumulated through tontines or deposits with trusted individuals. (The 1988 riots against the Maures in Senegal caused some disruption in urban informal savings since Senegalese tontines were often left for safe-keeping with Maure shopkeepers who disappeared during the exodus of the Maures from Senegal). There are some linkages between the formal and informal financial markets in Senegal, where the proceeds of tontines and village collective savings are sometimes put in banks for safekeeping while the formal financial intermediaries serve as conduits for emigrant remittances from France and elsewhere. In Zaire, some savings of informal sector operators are deposited in semi-formal cooperative accounts which then purchase government treasury bills. The deposits have been seriously eroded by inflation.

One of the anomalies of bank regulation in Senegal is that savings and loan associations are illegal since they are considered as banks, because they take deposits and make loans, but they cannot fulfill other regulations specified for banks[15]. The banking regulations will presumably be amended, during the current endeavour to restructure Senegal's banking system, to legalize saving and loan associations.

Parker Shipton makes the interesting point that in the Gambia there is a hierarchy of informal rural indebtedness: loans within villages including seasonal crop loans; share contracting arrangements; contributions for schooling and for labour migration with remittances expected in return later on; loans between small entrepreneurs; debts to relatives, neighbours, friends and merchants. In that hierarchy, "the newest, most distant, and least familiar lenders rank at the bottom"[16]. The last category includes the international agencies. Rural saving takes non-cash forms of livestock, food, jewellery, tools and household goods; cash savings are transformed as quickly as possible into tangible goods, in part to protect them from needy relatives and neighbours without appearing anti-social. The syndrome is typical for urban Africa as well. A vehicle frequently used for cash saving, particularly in urban areas, is the tontine (osusu in the Gambia) which operates on a regular basis (daily, weekly, 10-day, or monthly). At each interval, one member (whose turn in the rotation may be selected as a gamble) takes the whole amount. For a member whose turn comes early in the rotation the osusu is a credit mechanism; for one whose turn comes late in the rotation, it is a saving mechanism. Most of the rural osusus are composed of women who group themselves by age; in urban areas, the osusus include both sexes. The basic element of the osusu, collective responsibility of small groups for collection and repayment, is a feature that is now being incorporated into donor-funded projects.

An Ohio State University survey of informal rural finance in Niger in the mid-1980s found that 85 per cent of households had had access to informal credit from family, friends, relatives, merchants, tontines, and moneykeepers during the five years prior to the survey[17]. Wholesale merchants obtained loans from urban-based banks which they rechannelled to village retailers as consumer goods on consignment until the next harvest; the retailers sold the goods to villagers on credit which was repaid after the harvest and reimbursed on up the chain. Tontines varied in size and frequency of meetings: the smaller tontines involved small amounts and weekly meetings; the larger tontines involved market vendors, businessmen and professionals who met less frequently. Moneykeepers, usually merchants, kept deposits and served as pawn brokers; at the same time they made short-term loans. Contacts were frequent between moneykeepers and their clients which permitted the transformation of short into longer term loans.

Carl Liedholm emphasises the fact that, in addition to the money-lender, informal sources of credit for micro and small scale enterprises include advances of materials or cash from customers, supplier credit, and subcontracting[18]. Availability of credit from such sources depends partly on the reputation of the entrepreneur. Informal credit sources contribute mostly working capital to micro and small scale enterprises; they are not well suited to providing funds for fixed capital of growing firms. Formal credit institutions play a bigger role as micro-enterprises reach small and medium size.

A similar array of informal lending mechanisms (professional money lenders, informal credit arrangements tied to land, labour and marketing, voluntary credit societies and informal saving associations) plays a significant role in providing credit for small enterprises and households in Sri Lanka[19]. Urban retail vendors borrow by the day to pay for inputs needed for the day's transactions; traders and micro-producers borrow at somewhat longer term to finance stocks and current production. Voluntary credit groups include thrift and credit societies and *cheetus* (the Sri Lankan version of the tontine). Interest rates vary from zero to 350 per cent per year. Professional money lenders lend more for production purposes; interest-free lenders (friends and relatives) lend more for ceremonial purposes. In rural Sri Lanka, according to Nimal Sanderatne, the nature of informal lending is changing: interest rates charged by informal lenders are lower than is usually thought to be the case, a significant share of informal lending is for production purposes, and informal lenders try to secure their larger loans.

It is patently evident that the formal credit institutions cannot reach the clientele of the informal credit market because of the heavy costs of the formal credit bureaucracies and the tendency of informal borrowers to consider money from formal institutions as a gift rather than as a loan. There are essentially two alternatives open to aid donors and others for extending credit to informal sector enterprises: one is using NGOs as intermediaries, which is the basis of most informal credit projects; the other is to retail credit through the professional moneylenders, which most donors are reluctant to do because it smacks of usury. A scheme along the latter lines is being tried out since October 1988 in Sri Lanka where two state banks are extending loans to individuals "of proven creditworthiness" at 2.5 per cent per month (18 per cent per year) for on-lending in small amounts at 3.5 per cent per month (38 per cent per year), but the intermediaries complain that the one per cent per month margin is insufficient and the total volume of credit available from the banks is inadequate. Eventual success of the scheme will probably depend on the freedom left to the intermediaries to do their on-lending unhindered.

E. Technology for the Informal Sector

One of the virtues of the informal sector for those concerned with employment creation is the low capital cost per job in informal sector enterprises as compared with that in larger formal sector enterprise. The corollary is that productivity per worker and quality of output are usually considerably lower in the informal sector than in the formal. Increasing the productivity of informal sector enterprises and improving the quality of their output require the ability to adapt non-traditional technology and to introduce technological innovations and improvements.

Among the factors affecting the informal sector enterprise's ability to innovate are the extent of its dependence on foreign sources of equipment, and the level of education and training of the enterprise head. A review by Ajit Bhalla of informal sector enterprise experience with technological innovation found that relative autonomy from foreign technology and higher levels of education and training tended to encourage innovation[20]. Bhalla used two indicators of technological innovation: new product design; and domestic production of machinery. In that context, Bhalla cites Michigan State University studies on small (and micro) scale enterprises in West Africa that identified a considerable number of product changes as evidence of informal sector innovative capacity. Recent studies carried out for the ILO technology and employment research programme under Bhalla's direction showed varying rates of domestic production of machinery, which in fact are inter-correlated with the general technological level of the country. In Mali, many of the metalworking artisans surveyed had attempted to make their own machines but had failed because of lack of finance and/or lack of appropriate raw materials and equipment; prior experience in a formal sector enterprise appeared to be related to greater capacity for technological innovation[21]. In Ecuador, most of the machinery used by artisans producing metal grills for doors and windows was imported from abroad; the artisans limited their activity in that sphere to reproducing imported models and spare parts for repairing machines they own themselves; they did not produce spare parts for sale[22]. Constraints on machinery production included lack of working capital for testing prototypes and uncertainty of product demand. Many of the small producers covered in the Ecuador study acquired their technical competence working in larger-scale formal sector enterprises prior to establishing businesses on their own; they also had access to a state vocational training centre. In Bengalore (India), given the well-established capital goods sector in the country, most of the equipment used by the metalworking artisane was locally produced material available in the market; some was made by the artisans themselves.

F. Training for the Informal Sector

Many of the informal sector and micro-enterprise studies reviewed in Chapter 2 found that a majority of the self-employed informal sector enterprise heads acquired their skills on-the-job, as workers in formal sector enterprises or as apprentices in the informal sector, rather than in formal vocational training centres. In Africa, where the formal sector has been stagnating since the crises of the 1970s, where informal sector activities have expanded with the population, and where apprenticeship is the traditional mode of skills transmission, an increasing proportion of the self-employed are receiving their training as apprentices in the informal sector. In Latin America, there is a growing tendency for government institutions and NGOs to try to include informal sector participants in their formal training programmes[23].

It is often the case that the output of informal sector producers is of poor quality and that productivity is low, in part because of inadequate equipment and in part because of an insufficient level of technical skills. Lack of management skills reduces the operating efficiency of the micro-enterprises. A priori it is possible to inject improved skills into the formal vocational training and non-formal apprenticeship systems that produce informal sector entrepreneurs. How to go about such intervention without damaging the systems whose improvement is intended is an issue of considerable current interest[24].

Existing formal training institutions and programmes are inadequate from several points of view: except in Latin America, most of them provide training in skills and occupations that is intended to lead to employment in formal sector enterprises but that often does not correspond to opportunities in the informal sector; existing formal training programmes reach only a small proportion of the mass of new entrants to the labour market; they are primarily male-oriented whereas females make up a major share of informal sector participations; and the quality of training available in existing institutions is often not appropriate for preparing the trainees for productive work in either the formal or the informal sector. In Africa, using formal training institutions to enhance the training provided by master artisans to their apprentices may be a way to increase the effectiveness of both formal and non formal training. To design such training interventions, however, more needs to be known about existing patterns of non formal training. Obtaining such information is one of the aims of the on-going World Bank-ILO-OECD Development Centre research project on Education and Training for Skills and Income in the Urban Informal Sector in Sub-Saharan Africa[25].

The indigenous apprenticeship system is of great importance in Africa because it provides vocational training for the majority of the urban labour force, many of whom are in any case left out of the formal educational system, at no cost to the governments of the countries concerned. It also serves the social function of integrating teen-age (and older) youths into the life of work and of reducing somewhat the extent of delinquency in the cities. In most cases, the families of the apprentices pay at least nominal fees to the master artisan. There are, however, some significant differences in systems of payments by apprentices (or their families) for training and payments by the artisans to apprentices for work done during the training period. In their June 1989 survey of Ibadan (Nigeria) for the above-mentioned World Bank-ILO-OECD Development Centre project, Stace Birks and Clive Sinclair found that only 10 per cent of the masters took on apprentices without charging a fee as compared with the two-thirds that Callaway found to be the case in the 1960s; fees were offset by a combination of payments in cash and kind (pocket money and free board and lodging) estimated at twice the amount of the fees. In Madagascar, so say the experts, the only apprentices who receive any real training are members of the extended family of the master; non-family apprentices have the real status of underpaid hired workers. In Lomé (Togo), apprenticeship fees have become such a major part of the income of some of the artisans that their shops look more like vocational training schools than production units. Several of the artisanal associations (e.g., the hairdressers) have set minimum fees for apprenticeship training to be charged by their members. The government, on its side, has issued regulations that include a set of maximum fees that in some cases are lower than the minimum fees the artisans want to impose.

To paraphrase Kenneth King, contributions to the development of skills, attitudes and awareness in the informal sector can be made by formal education and training institutions, by NGOs, and by private non-formal training[26]. The problem for training policy makers and practioners is how to integrate the several sources of training.

G. Regulation and Informality

The extent of legislation regulating small scale economic activity varies from country to country. Regulations are established for a variety of reasons, among them that their elite groups like their cities to be clean, neat and well-run but more often to protect existing or would-be economic, social or racial vested interests. Lima's myriad regulations as described by de Soto were established fundamentally to protect the cities of the urban elites from being invaded by the rural masses, the *campesinos*, and secondarily to protect the economic prerogatives of merchants, formal sector transport operators and other producers already well established in the urban market. The laws regulating residence and economic activity in Port Moresby (Papua-New Guinea) were written by European-Australian colonists to keep native Papua-New Guineans out of the city. The regulations written to reinforce colonial economic interests in West Africa were added to by the newly independent nationalist governments trying to protect local import-substituting industries, newly created state enterprises, and untenable foreign exchange regimes whose dismantlement has only recently begun.

The extent to which restrictive legislation is enforced also varies widely, in part because of differences in the socio-political framework from one country to another. How the bureaucracy see its own interests also affects how the regulations are administered. Many regulations and controls continue to exist, whatever their original rationale, because they create a climate favorable to bribery of government agents empowered to enforce the regulations. Eades has pointed out that legislation regulating trade has provided considerable discretionary power to government officials who, in many instances, "may well decide that regular payoffs... are preferable to over-zealous enforcement of the law"[27]. In West Africa, enforcement of regulations is weakened where officials (or their wives or close kin) are part-time businessmen themselves and where social networks of small-scale entrepreneurs and State agents overlap. In Singapore, by contrast, the bureaucracy has been educated in English-medium schools and has become sufficiently divorced from communal and extended family ties that corruption is rare and regulations are severely enforced.

The recent accent on surreptitious avoidance of regulation as a key feature of informality, since the publicity received by Hernando de Soto's *The Other Path*, has several interesting implications. One is the *reductio ad absurdum* that if all regulations were abrogated, informality would cease to exist. The real question is which regulations are illegitimate obstructions to informal sector economic activity rather than a useful and rational framework for such activity. De Soto's central proposition, that eliminating predatory licensing and other useless regulations will liberate dynamic capitalist activity by the energetic poor, has to be balanced by consideration of which regulations are legitimate and should therefore be enforced.

Another implication of the identification of informality with avoidance of regulations is that the concept of informality is not limited to micro scale enterprises but extends to larger scale operators who also find that direct or indirect avoidance of regulatory requirements and taxes greatly improves their net profit position. Since larger scale enterprises are visible to the regulatory authorities, avoidance is carried out indirectly through subcontracting to smaller scale and micro-enterprises. Policy makers have therefore to ask themselves two interrelated questions: a) Should there be a double standard for enforcement of regulations depending on size of the enterprise involved, strict for larger enterprises and less strict for small and micro scale enterprises? b) If a double standard is acceptable, how far down along the subcontracting chain should strict enforcement be applied?

H. Informality in Developed Countries

The "underground economy" of Western Europe and the United States has a strong family resemblance to the informal sector of the Third World. Self-employed builders, carpenters, plumbers and vehicle repairmen start small enterprises that operate outside the tax net, doing business on a cash basis and leaving no accounting records. Garment manufacturing sweatshops produce ready-mode clothing for merchant-capitalists in apartments and lofts in Paris, Berlin, New York, Miami and other big cities with large immigrant populations. Sub-contractors to larger firms work out of shops in the garages or the basements of their homes to minimize capital and operating outlays. Such enterprises usually stay small in order to keep out of sight of labour code inspectors and tax collectors until they can accumulate the ressources to expand their scale of operation and are convinced that functioning above-ground will be profitable enough to comply with labour and tax regulations. In this context, we define the underground economy to exclude clearly criminal activity such as drugs and prostitution. In Italy, the 1980s witnessed significant growth in industrial production and in exports of industrial goods produced by small and medium scale enterprises operating at least partly outside the tax net and the system of labour regulations, with the tacit approval of the government authorities concerned with reducing unemployment and with maintaining the competitivity of Italy's exports.

The Italian experience with quasi-informal industrial production has been especially significant in Emilia-Romagna where the regional and local authorities, controlled by the Italian Communist Party after World War II, implemented a policy of support for small enterpreneurs of local peasant and working class origins[28]. The transition from agriculture to industry, which occurred during the 1950-1970 period, was based on the development of networks of small and medium scale enterprises in the metallurgical, mechanical, garment and textile branches. The enterprises sub-contracted work to each other but they all remained small to medium scale. In the 1970s and 1980s, there was also a significant expansion of small scale service sector enterprises, including tourism along the Adriatic coast, which produced a lower rate of unemployment in Emilia-Romagna than in the rest of Italy. Parallel to a general increase in the level of education and training, there is a growing tendency for students to work part-time as informals (while being recorded in official statistics as seeking work). It has been estimated that 18 per cent of the employed male labour force in Emilia-Romagna were informals (the same percentage as in Italy as a whole). The corresponding figure for females was 38 per cent in Emilia-Romagna (and 49 per cent in Italy as a whole). The contribution of the informal economy to the gross regional product was estimated at 12 per cent for Emilia-Romagna (and 10.5 per cent for the gross national product of Italy as a whole).

A recent estimate puts the contribution of the "black economy" in the ECE countries as a whole in 1985 at 4 per cent of gross domestic product, with many qualifications as to the methods of its derivation[29].

Maintaining a competitive edge is a basic driving force for most of the evasion of taxes and regulations that characterizes informality in the developed country context as described in the provocative collection of studies on the informal economy in advanced and less developed countries edited by Alejandro Portes, Manuel Castells and Lauren A. Benton[30]. In Spain, informalization spreads as formal sector firms seek exemptions from labour legislation in order to meet the competition from firms that have already gone underground[31]. In New York City, unlicensed and unregistered informal production, which occurs in all forty SIC (standard industrial classification) sectors, is located mostly in densely populated areas with high shares of immigrants (Hispanic, Chinese, Korean, and newly arrived East Europeans). Up-grading ("gentrification") of some old residential and commercial areas has forced traditional garment industry sweatshops to more outlying areas of the city; in some cases, the space vacated is now occupied by higher-quality informal enterprise activities such as cabinet-making workshops and sweater-knitting mills[32]. Miami (Florida) has two informal sectors (in addition to drug-running and money-laundering which we are defining as criminal rather than informal): one organised by middle class Cuban immigrant entrepreneurs who employ mostly Cuban immigrant workers at low wages; and the other an informal sector of low income immigrant Haitians based upon casual self-employment. The Cuban community is integrated into Miami's garment industry, construction, and hotels and restaurants. Haitian women are petty traders, food preparers and dressmakers; Haitian men provide semi-skilled services in construction and in automobile repair and provide informal transport to Haitian daily agricultural labourers working on farms within long commuting distance from Miami[33]. Enforcement of regulations by the tax authorities and the US Department of Labour is sporadic and probably half-hearted since informality is recognized as an essential survival strategy for new arrivals in the US; but at some point the US authorities may have to take a conscious decision as to where to draw the line between areas in which evasion is tolerable because enforcement would severely worsen the situation of the informal sector participants and areas where it is intolerable because evasion threatens the integrity of the system of social legislation.

Easten Europe's new economic order creates still another facet of informality. Former black marketeers are now budding entrepreneurs. New systems of supply, marketing and pricing are emerging rapidly. Large scale open unemployment will push more individuals into self-employment and small scale enterprise activity. It will be interesting to see what contribution micro and small enterprise activity make to the restructuring of Eastern Europe's economies and what contribution the dismantling of the restrictive panoply of regulations makes to renewed economic growth.

Notes and References

1. BREMER-FOX (1989).
2. BROMLEY (1978).
3. Mc GEE (1973); and Mc GEE and YEUNG (1977).
4. See the Chapter on "Informal Housing" in DE SOTO (1989).
5. EVERS (1981).
6. GROWN (1989).
7. TINKER (1985).
8. BERGER (1989).
9. TENDLER (1989).
10. POSNER (1983).
11. See the excellent set of papers prepared for the Ohio State University seminar on *Informal Financial Markets in Development*, sponsored by the World Bank and A.I.D. and held in Washington, D.C., October 18-20, 1989.
12. GERMIDIS, KESSLER and MEGHIR (1989).
13. SCHREIDER and CUEVAS (1989).
14. FLAMMANG (1989) and ARTHUR YOUNG ASSOCIATES (1989).
15. ZAROUR (1988).
16. SHIPTON (1989).
17. GRAHAM (1989).
18. LIEDHOLM (1989).
19. SANDERATNE (1989).
20. BHALLA (1989).
21. CAPT (1987).
22. FARRELL (1989).
23. GUERRERO (1989).
24. FLUITMAN (1989b)
25. See the following documents of the joint World Bank (Education and Training Division, Africa Technical Department), ILO (Vocational Training Branch, Training Department), and OECD Development Centre Research Project on Education and Training for Skills and Income in the Urban Informal Sector in Sub-Saharan Africa: *The Study Outline*, October 5, 1989; BIRK and SINCLAIR with FLUITMAN (1989); and VARDON, JAROUSSE and MINGAT (1989). The results of a field survey carried out in Lomé (Togo) in November-December 1989 are being written up by Fred Fluitman and Xavier Oudin. The project managers for the three collaborating institutions are Bernard Salomé for the World Bank, Fred Fluitman for the ILO, and David Turnham for the OECD Development Centre.

26. KING (1989).
27. EADES (1985).
28. CAPECCHI (1989).
29. WILLARD (1989).
30. PORTES, CASTELLS and BENTON (1989).
31. YBARRA (1989).
32. SASSEN-KOOB (1989).
33. STEPICK (1989).

Chapter 6

THE INFORMAL SECTOR IN THE 1990s

A. Lessons Learned Since the 1972 ILO Kenya Employment Mission Report

As pointed out frequently above, most of what we know about the informal sector was contained in embryo in the 1972 ILO Kenya Employment Mission Report[1]. We have, nevertheless, learned a good deal since then about the behaviour of the informal sector in various parts of the developing world, as demonstrated in the recently published report of the 1988 OECD Development Centre seminar on *The Informal Sector Revisited*[2] and in the earlier chapters of the present volume. Several features are worth highlighting.

1. The Informal Sector is Here to Stay

One of the most obvious lessons learned since 1972 is that informal activities, defined primarily as micro-enterprise activities, are expanding rather than withering away. That is happening both in situations where economic activity of the formal sector is contracting (as in much of sub-Saharan Africa) and where it is expanding (as in some of the newly industrializing countries of Asia and Latin America): where the formal economy contracts, more individuals are pushed into informal sector activities for lack of alternative ways of earning a living; where the formal economy expands, it creates direct and indirect demands for goods and services produced by the informal sector and thereby draws more individuals into informal sector activities. It is still a reasonable hypothesis that if and when economic development accelerates enough to absorb most of the new labour force entrants into formal sector activity, micro-scale enterprise activity will diminish in relative if not absolute terms; but that is not yet the case. In the meanwhile, most of the surveys summarized in Chapter 2 above have reported that a majority of informal sector participants prefer the relative independence their occupations offer to the status of low-paid formal sector factory workers. It is probably true that earnings in the informal sector are in general lower than in the formal sector, but enough of the self-employed artisans and traders earn more than the official minimum wage (or even the average formal sector wage) to entice others to continue to try their luck as informal micro-entrepreneurs.

In the aggregate, informality might appear to be solely a consequence of a surplus of labour in a narrow market, an unsatisfactory alternative to open unemployment. In that vein, the scenario postulated by the Harris-Todaro model of the 1970s was one in which the urban informal sector was primarily a queue for rural to urban migrants looking for formal sector jobs. In fact, however, the ILO and other informal sector surveys showed that many informal sector participants who had worked in the formal sector before going into the the informal sector shifted to the informal sector not because they were redundant to the formal sector but because they chose to be self-employed, using skills acquired in the formal sector to establish themselves as independent producers or traders; they were small scale entrepreneurs who chose self-employment because they could capitalize on skills (and savings) acquired in the formal sector. Other informals stayed in the informal sector because they had received their training in an informal sector activity in which they could continue to make a living. In most programmes for support of informal sector activity, it is now accepted that the micro-enterprise is essentially a viable economic institution and that participants are not trying to escape from informality.

There are two related questions concerning the evolution of the informal sector that have not been answered by the surveys cited in Chapter 2. The first is the extent to which individual micro-enterprises grow into small and medium scale firms and become formal, at least as defined by size. The surveys identify only existing micro-enterprises but not former micro-enterprises that are no longer to be found, either because they have failed or because they have grown to small or medium scale and are not recognizable as ex-informals. The second question is what happens to the informal sector in a country experiencing an economic boom because all the elements for vigorous economic growth have come together, in particular appropriate macro-economic policies and a buoyant world market for the country's exports. For industrial production, the Korean case is instructive: according to Ian Little, Dipak Mazumdar and John Page[3], during the period from 1963 to 1975, over 86 per cent of the one million persons absorbed into manufacturing employment went into establishments with over 100 workers while establishments with 5 to 9 workers (the smallest size group recorded) showed no change in employment.

The impact of the economic crisis of the 1980s on the informal sector has been mixed. In Senegal, for example, urban self-employment and informal sector activity expanded in part because the number of formal sector jobs declined in the face of a continued expansion of the urban labour force. At the same time, the shut-down of some formal sector industrial plants (such as the Bata shoe factory in Dakar) created a market opening for informal sector production of consumer goods. In Nigeria, recent severe foreign exchange shortages and subsequent devaluations of the currency as a structural adjustment measure severely constrained formal sector access to imported raw materials and reduced formal sector output; the result was a boom in informal sector production, the classic example being soap of which artisanal output increases rapidly whenever shortages of imported raw materials cripple formal sector production[4]. In the more industrialized Third World countries such as Mexico, it would appear that informalisation through subcontracting spread during the economic crisis as formal sector plants tried to reduce costs in order to meet intensified competition, but that informalisation continued to spread during economic recovery as well since formal sector plant managers have become accustomed to the subcontracting mode of plant management[5].

There is another aspect of expanding informality that is definitional, as analysts extend the theoretical range of informality by focusing on avoidance of regulations as its key element. Avoidance of regulations is not limited to micro-entrepreneurs but is also a feature of small and medium scale enterprise activity and (if the firms can get away with it) of large scale enterprise activity as well. On that definition, what might be called creeping informality is on the march.

2. Competition and Complementarity Between the Informal and Formal Sectors

Informal sector activity is both competitive with and complementary to the level of activity of the formal economy. Informal sector commodity producers compete with formal sector producers of (usually) lower quality and lower cost consumer goods. Street vendors compete with formal sector retail stores. Informal sector transport competes successfully with formal sector bus companies, often because the informal sector taxi and minibus owners have a greater incentive than formal sector employees to keep their vehicles in good enough repair to keep them on the road.

The informal and formal industrial sectors are complementary in their subcontracting inter-relationships in a number of countries, more frequently in Latin America and in Asia than in Africa. In addition, the formal sector is usually the supplier of inputs to the informal sector producers and traders, either directly or through intermediary formal sector traders. Even in street-vending, which is normally keenly competitive with formal sector retailers, it has been shown in Santiago (Chile)[6] and elsewhere that the street vendors often obtain their input supplies from friendly retailers and other distributors who see the street vendors as a means of increasing their own turnover rather than as competitors.

For many years, the Japanese experience with subcontracting from larger to smaller enterprises has been proposed as a model for the developing economies. In fact, subcontracting by formal sector enterprises to informal sector enterprises is, in some Latin America and Asian developing countries, already a major source of demand for informal sector outputs; in other countries, particularly in Africa, that kind of subcontracting is much less prevalent. However, it is often difficult to identify the networks of subcontracting through the labyrinth of semi-clandestinity that characterizes much of informal sector activity.

The known patterns of subcontracting are often complex, cascading from large (sometimes multinational) enterprises to smaller firms to backyard informal sector enterprises to household workers. The individual entrepreneur or household worker will often be dealing only with an intermediary and will not know at all who his or her ultimate customer is. Research in such instances has to take on an air of detective work. A household survey can identify informal sector participants and define their areas of activity while an informal sector establishment survey can throw light on the direct customers of the informal sector enterprise, but neither will be sufficient to describe the chain of forward linkages of the informal sector accurately. The linkages can really be traced only backward from the formal sector; if the various links in the chain are willing to provide information on the entities to whom they are subcontracting. The further into informality the enquiry goes, the less precise is the information likely to become.

Subcontracting down the chain takes place as a method of cutting costs, in the first instance by the formal sector enterprise that avoids the fixed costs and social charges attached to direct employment of a large labour force and then by successive layers of subcontractors, each of whom tries to reduce the costs to his own enterprise by squeezing the margin of the next producer in the chain. Exploitation of the weaker links in the chain in the relatively free market of the informal sector is one of the implicit characteristics of the system.

At a more egalitarian level, subcontracting within the informal sector is typical of city districts where micro-enterprises congregate, be they in a metropolis like Calcutta or Cairo, or in a smaller city like Dakar. An appropriate image to describe the phenomenon is an informal assembly line operating down a street of interlinked micro-enterprises.

3. Policies and Policy Changes

The informal sector has usually faced a negatively or openly hostile policy environment. The impact of macro-economic policy is frequently negative, while open hostility is often the case at the micro level. Nevertheless, there has been recent movement toward developing and applying positive policies in support of informal sector activity.

The elements of macro-economic policy that were most criticized by the ILO employment missions of the 1970s were tariff and quantitative protection of large scale local enterprises and the implicit and explicit subsidies provided to them through allocations of foreign exchange, in the face of gross overvaluation of the local currency, and allocations of credit at subsidized interest rates. Informal sector enterprises, which did not have direct access to such largesse, were in that respect faced with unfair competition. The structural adjustment programmes of the 1980s modified or cancelled a number of the special advantages received by the formal sector as quantitive restrictions were removed, tariffs were lowered, currencies were devalued, and (in some instances) interest rates were raised. In many instances, the changes affected informal sector producers favourably in spite of (or because of) the difficulties faced by the formal sector as a result of structural adjustment. The closing of some formal sector businesses created opportunities for informal sector producers that earlier had been virtually wiped out by formal sector competition.

Government policies aimed directly at the informal sector in the 1970s were generally hostile; they were typified by police harassment of street vendors and artisans working in the central city. Harassment has in many cases been reduced in recent years as the productive contributions of the informal sector have come to be recognized, but government attitudes are still basically hostile because the informal sector, since it is productive, is now viewed primarily as a potential source of increased tax collections and informal sector participants are seen as tax evaders (even though they are in reality already a major contributor to municipal finances through marketplace fees and business license fees). Getting governments to take a positive attitude toward the informal sector is still a major challenge.

4. Effectiveness of Support Programmes: Minimalist Versus Package Programmes

The focus of most programmes in support of informal sector activity has been credit and technical assistance to producers of goods and services in what Georges Nihan called the "modern" informal sector. Occasionally such programmes also provide support to small traders with fixed places of business.

The constraints faced by micro-enterprises in production and services have been identified over and over again. As expressed by the entrepreneurs, their major difficulty is lack of liquidity: they have little or no access to bank credit; and their profits are infrequently sufficient to generate much business or personal saving. In reality, the lack of liquidity that they perceive may be only a reflection of more fundamental problems of management and the business climate that they may or may not recognize. The evidence is, however, that access to credit provided by government or donor programmes to functioning micro-enterprises does result in increased production and sales and therefore in increased profits, so that the question whether lack of liquidity is a first cause or a symptom of something deeper loses some of its relevance.

The difficulty with the credit programmes created so far is that most of them are still pilot projects with limited funding, which has two consequences: they are expensive to manage (which is one reason why the banks normally do not lend to micro-enterprises in the first place); and it may be that the return to capital of the entrepreneurs who do receive loans is relatively high because there are so few of them. It is not clear what would be the consequences of a massive increase in the availability of credit to micro-enterprises in given market situations.

Increased productivity also implies disturbance of the low-level equilibrium of the market for informal sector outputs. Programmes directed at increasing productivity through improved technology or through improved training (or both) will improve the situation of the informal sector participants who receive the technology and training relative to the others who do not. Only confidence that increased supply (and improved quality of that supply) will also increase demand justifies the programmes from the point of view of the welfare of the aggregate of micro-producers.

We know that technical assistance to micro (and small) enterprises by governments, international agencies and NGOs is expensive; but there are several views on the extent of the benefits derived. The technical assistance menu includes basic advice on business management, some technology transfer, and vocational training. There are several views on how much technical assistance the informal sector really needs and the forms it should take. The professionals in each of the fields just mentioned are convinced of the importance and the value of their contributions. The professional purveyors of credit are convinced of the value of their own contribution and take a more skeptical view of that of the others. Another view has emerged from the ILO/Swiss Cooperation project on support to the informal sector in francophone Africa which has found that the micro-entrepreneurs soon become aware of their specific requirements for technical assistance and will ask for it when they need it[7].

The ILO/Swiss Cooperation programme is effective in reaching micro-entrepreneurs. The programme, with antennae in Mali (Bamako and four other towns), Rwanda (Kigali and three other towns), and Togo (Lomé and three other towns), helps informal sector producers to organize themselves, channels small amounts of funding to informal sector producers, and provides access to training and technology on request. The programme has been successful in achieving its immediate aims of sensitising and organizing artisans at the grassroots level, but it is limited in scale. Replication is labour-intensive and building relations at the grassroots level is a slow process.

An evaluation of 32 USAID micro-enterprise development projects in 10 countries, published in draft in March 1989, provides a number of insights into the impact of technical cooperation related to the informal sector[8]. The strongest finding is that minimalist direct assistance programs that aim to improve the performance of micro-enterprises by providing short-term credit without attempting to transform the micro-enterprises into more complex businesses have a better record of success to date than do more ambitious programs. However, the needs of the vast majority of micro-enterprises cannot be met merely by providing small loans for working capital. Unfortunately, understanding and application of technical assistance and training to micro-enterprise development are far less advanced than for credit. In the view of the USAID evaluators, technical assistance and training programs should be designed to respond to identified business needs of micro-entrepreneurs. In that connection, the joint World Bank/ILO/OECD Development Centre project on Education and

Training for Skills and Income in the Urban Informal Sector in Sub-Saharan Africa currently under way is examining ways to use education and training to improve the skills of both artisans and apprentices in the informal sector.

The present situation thus appears to present the following scenario. Extension to micro-enterprises of government training and technical assistance activities (such as those of Colombia's SENA) is viewed with suspicion by the potential recipients of assistance. Training and technical assistance provided by the international donor community and by NGOs are accepted and appreciated by micro-entrepreneurs, but the volume of resources is limited and projects stay pretty much on a pilot scale. The programme challenge for developing country governments is two-fold: to gain the confidence of the informal sector participants concerned; and to ensure sufficient government budget finance to make the programmes effective.

B. Where Do We Go From Here?

1. Further Extension of Informality

It is a good bet that informality will spread during the 1990s in both of its two main aspects: informality as embodied in the micro-enterprise; and informality as the avoidance of regulations.

Micro-scale informal sector enterprises will continue to proliferate in the Third World during the 1990s because the manpower absorptive capacity of urban formal sector activities will not keep pace with the increase in the urban labour force, and self-employment and micro-enterprise activity will have to fill the gap. The supply of labour is already determined by the demography of the past decade and even in the unlikely event that Third World birth rates were to decline sharply in the 1990s, the working population for the decade is already born. The labour force increase will be slowed only a little by AIDS-induced increases in death rates. The demand for labour may be expected to rise as the world economy recovers from the crises of the past decade, but formal sector absorption of labour in the Third World will nevertheless be limited by high capital costs per job, by the diversion of international investment (and international aid for the next five years) to Central and Eastern Europe, and the fall from favour of the state economic enterprise as a panacea for Third World development. Indigenous growth will come about through the expansion of small and micro-scale activity.

Informality defined as avoidance of regulations will be affected by two opposing trends: elimination of many of the unnecessary and anti-economic regulations that now impede the "natural" expansion of small and micro-scale activity; and continued pressure on formal sector enterprises to reduce costs of production by avoiding labour and health regulations and taxes, either directly through fraud or indirectly through sub-contracting to smaller enterprises. Elimination of the "bad" regulations will reduce the scope of informality by definition and it will encourage small enterprise activity. Avoidance of taxes and of labour and health regulations by larger scale enterprises will be reduced only by intensified enforcement, not by any change of heart on the part of formal sector entrepreneurs.

2. The Regulatory Framework

A typical regulatory system contains the following elements, all of which affect the informal sector directly or indirectly: regulations concerning legal access to property; a license from the state or local authority to function as a business in a given work place; minimum standards of hygiene for the work place and for the output of the enterprise; minimum wages and limitations on the firing of workers; minimum standards for physical infrastructure and buildings for housing and business premises; national and local taxes on property and income and (usually local) taxes on business permits; and application of formal accounts to enterprise operations. Concern for informal sector activity leads to two types of questions: a) which regulations are economically and socially justified (and should be continued) and which are unjustified (and should be eliminated); and b) which otherwise desirable regulations could be suspended as part of an effort to encourage informal sector economic activity?

The effect of the regulatory framework of the economy on the informal sector was a major concern of the ILO Kenya Employment Mission of 1972[9], which focused on the one-sided protection and subsidies provided by governments to the formal sector from which the informal sector was excluded, while the informal sector's day to day operations were being sporadically harassed by the police. Interest in the topic was intensified during the 1980s by Hernando de Soto's demonstrations of the effects of the dead hand of Peruvian regulations in *The Other Path*[10], although there are a number of countries where national and local regulations affecting the operations of the informal sector are almost non-existent. De Soto's analyses focused on the rigidity of the exclusionary practices which are being progressively and successfully by-passed by the informal sector but at great social and economic cost. Since 1988, the ILO has commissioned a number of country studies in Latin America to estimate the costs of legalizing informal sector activity, and in Africa to analyze existing legislation affecting artisanal activity and the extent to which the legislation is enforced; the results of the studies are not yet available. The OECD Development Centre is examining the relations between the informal sector and national administrative and political authorities as part of the project on Governance and Entrepreneurship in its 1990-1992 Programme of Research[11]. The Africa Bureau of the US Agency for International Development considers the regulatory framework as a central theme of its work with micro-enterprises and the informal sector[12]. The World Bank's Africa Technical Department has generated a research proposal for an Africa Regional Programme on Enterprise Development that has the business environment and the regulatory framework as a major component[13]. The elements of the regulatory framework identified in the World Bank's research proposal include the following: barriers to entry; labour market regulations; marketing and distribution controls; regulations governing land ownership and tenure; financial market regulations; fiscal regulations; factor mobility regulations; legal and commercial codes; and traditional laws and social customs.

It is clear that the regulatory framework hampers development of informal sector activities, but also that there is a need to maintain a certain degree of social order in the cities for the good of the community. A case where the interests of the informal sector participants and their customers are clearly in conflict with those of the community is in urban transport. The informal urban collective taxis and minibuses provide an important service but they also add immeasurably to the traffic chaos of Lima (to take de Soto's example), while the poor state of repair of many of the vehicles adds to the dangers of urban transport to life and limb. There are undoubtedly solutions to be found, but complete deregulation is not one of them.

The new wave of studies cited above will need to focus on the two aspects of regulation when examining specific situations in the 1990s: the elements of the regulatory framework that hamper development of the informal sector; and extent to which regulation is justified by concern for the good of the community. It is patently absurd that nine months of pushing papers through a government bureaucracy are required in order to establish a legal micro-scale factory, as cited by de Soto. It is perhaps less absurd to attempt to maintain some measure of control over street traders (and pickpockets) in the main streets of a capital city, or over informal collective transport using the city's streets.

The applications of labour regulations to the informal sector is a particularly sensitive issue for organizations such as the ILO and its national Labour Ministry constituents which have been concerned with devising and negotiating labour standards for the last three quarters of a century but are also concerned with the creation of productive employment and with reducing unemployment. In many instances, informality is a technique for avoiding the costs of meeting government-prescribed labour standards. The lower labour costs that result often make the difference between the financial viability or non-viability of a micro-enterprise. Should such informal sector enterprises in a developing country therefore be exempted *de jure* from such regulations, which they already avoid *de facto*, in order to promote employment and production? Even if the answer is positive for the Third World, since the same kind of informality is now spreading in the older industrialized countries as well, particularly among their new immigrant communities[14], the question of what degree of competitive non-compliance with labour regulations is to be condoned by the authorities in New York, Miami, Paris and London is now and will continue to be posed in the developed countries.

3. Informal Finance

Lack of credit is generally the major constraint on their productive activity that informal sector entrepreneurs perceive, yet there is evidence that considerable volumes of informal savings exist at the local community level in the hands of traditional moneylenders and money "keepers", in rotating savings and loan groups such as tontines, and in individual cash hiding places. Most informal sector enterprises are initially financed out of the personal savings of the entrepreneur or the entrepreneur's family, but most of the cash accumulated in rotating savings schemes and most loans issued by moneylenders are used for ceremonial and other consumption purposes. As more gets to be known about informal sources of saving and credit, however, it is likely that they will be progressively integrated into circuits financing productive activity. For groups of small entrepreneurs in the same line of business whose members contribute to tontines, there are already examples of the use of such funds for productive purposes (usually for working capital) either as direct loans to members from the rotating pot or as a guaranty for formal bank loans to members of the group; and the movement may be expected to grow. Like much informal activity, most changes and growth in informal finance will come about spontaneously. However, there is room for outside intervention of two sorts: positive changes in regulations to legalize rotating saving and credit associations where their legality is in question; and assistance in organizing saving and credit associations from institutions such as the World Council of Credit Unions. The 1990s will see both a growth of informal finance and its integration into semi-formal systems.

4. Policies and Programmes

The policy climate for the informal sector of the 1990s is more favourable than in the past as a consequence both of the wave of World Bank-fostered structural adjustment programmes of the 1980s and of the increased interest in the informal sector on the part of the international agencies and national governments. Macro-economic policies have been modified to reduce tariff protection, to remove quantitative restrictions, and to adjust overvalued exchange rates, thereby reducing the value of exemptions that larger firms but not small and informal sector enterprises were able to obtain. To some extent, nominal interest rates have been raised above price inflation rates to arrive at positive real interest rates, thereby reducing implicit subsidies to capital. Perverse ceilings on interest rates to small scale enterprises, perverse in that the effect of such ceilings is to reduce the availability of credit to small scale enterprises, are falling out of fashion. Governments have begun to modify public hiring and wage policies to discourage candidates for public sector jobs and thereby to encourage self-employment. Fewer costly and loss-making public sector enterprises are being created and many existing ones have been put on the market for privatization although with varying degrees of success. As a result of the policy shifts noted, implicit discrimination against small and micro-scale enterprises is being markedly reduced.

Other positive policy changes in favour of small and micro scale enterprises are also likely. Changes in banking regulations to legalize and to facilitate business-oriented savings and loan associations are to be expected. The easing of regulatory constraints sought by Hernando de Soto in the spheres of housing and urban transport will result from public and internal political pressure. Simplification of bureaucratic procedures affecting small scale business activity is inevitable as a result of the current onslaught of research and publicity concerning the regulatory framework, although the process will be resisted by underpaid government officials who can now supplement their salaries by exacting bribes to grease the machinery of regulation. In that context, elimination of regulations, where possible, will be the best sort of simplification from the enterprise point of view.

Another policy area likely to come into its own in the next few years, especially in Africa, will be the restructuring of government purchasing systems to favour small scale enterprises by seeking out potential suppliers and by writing sizeable price preferences for small scale domestic producers into the bidding procedures for government contracts. A variant will be to reorganize public building and works programmes so that they can be carried out through small scale sub-contractors along the principles of the World Bank's Senegal Public Works and Employment project of 1989[15]. Redirecting the implementation of public works projects toward small scale building contractors will be particularly significant for donor-financed programmes if the fashion swings away from structural adjustment programmes and back to infrastructure projects as a major vehicle for the transfer of resources to aid recipient countries.

This brings us back to the demand side of the policy framework, which was fundamental to the PREALC approach to the informal sector discussed in Chapters 2 and 3 above and which was emphasized in the 1988 UNDP/Government of the Netherlands/ILO/UNIDO report on *Development of Rural Small Industrial Enterprise*[16] and more recently by Roger Teszler and Klaas Molenaar in their search for new Dutch approaches to small enterprise development[17]. Government bidding procedures are relevant in general but are particularly important if resources are available for re-stimulating depressed national economies through government spending programmes (included those financed by the international donors). A macro-economic policy environment that includes demand creation enhanced by development of infrastructure requires financial resources that the developing countries presumably lack. Since the prospects for increased international aid flows are not bright, availability of such resources in 1990s will depend on a general revival of the world economy and, with that, a general improvement in world prices of the Third World's export commodities.

5. Research Agendas for the 1990s

A wide range of research related to informal sector activities is already under way or has been proposed by the international agencies. As noted earlier, the World Bank-ILO-OECD Development Centre research programme on Education and Training for Skills and Income in the Urban Informal Sector in Africa is partly completed. The World Bank's Africa Regional Technical Department has proposed a $900 000 Africa Regional Programme on Enterprise Development research and development programme covering a number of major topics: the business environment and regulatory framework; technical services support systems; financial support systems; the dynamics of enterprise development; inter-generational patterns of enterprise development; a review of pilot schemes for micro, small and medium scale enterprise development in selected countries and sectors; and a review of NGO/PVO assistance for enterprise development. The GEMINI (Growth and Equity Through Micro-Enterprise Investments and Institutions) programme of the US Agency for International Development's Science and Technology Bureau has the following major themes: micro-enterprise growth and dynamics; economic and social impacts of assistance to micro-enterprises; subsector analysis and assistance; improvement in delivery of nonfinanical assistance; institutional alternatives and institutional strengthening; expanding opportunities for women in micro-enterprises; and scaling-up of micro-enterprise programmes. As noted earlier, Christian Morrisson is developing the Governance and Enterprise component of the OECD Development Centre's 1990-1992 Programme of Research. In 1990, the US Agency for International Development's Africa Bureau was focusing part of its research effort on the formulation of an informal sector-related strategy for enterprise development in the Sahel.

Three obvious candidates for future research might be added to the extended agendas cited above: a) As the geographical range of intervention programmes expands and other international, national or NGO support programmes are formulated, what is now standard information will be needed on existing informal sector activities in specific localities not yet studied. In addition, it would be interesting to investigate the histories of small and medium scale enterprises to identify those that started as informal micro-enterprises and subsequently moved into the formal sector. b) Within the new research on the supportive and inhibitory effects of the regulatory framework on informal sector activities, a specific aspect will have to be the implications for labour legislation of the increasing informalisation of parts of the production processes of formal sector manufacturing enterprises in the newly industrializing countries. c) The present approach of the international aid agencies toward the informal sector concentrates on its best-off components, potentially viable productive enterprises. Greater attention should perhaps be devoted now to what Michael Farbman and Alan Lessik[18] call survival activities of the poorest as distinct from micro-enterprise activity.

Notes and References

1. ILO (1972).
2. TURNHAM, SALOME and SCHWARZ (1990).
3. LITTLE, MAZUMDAR and PAGE (1987).
4. BIRKS and SINCLAIR with FLUITMAN (1989).
5. ROBERTS (1989).
6. TOKMAN.
7. MALDONADO (1989).
8. US AGENCY FOR INTERNATIONAL DEVELOPMENT (1989).
9. ILO (1972).
10. DE SOTO (1989).
11. OECD DEVELOPMENT CENTRE (1989).
12. BREMER-FOX (1989).
13. WORLD BANK (1990).
14. PORTES, CASTELLS and BENTON (1989).
15. WORLD BANK (1989).
16. UNDP/GOVERNMENT OF NETHERLANDS/ILO/UNIDO (1988).
17. TESZLER and MOLENAAR (1989).
18. FARBMAN and LESSIK (1989).

BIBLIOGRAPHY

AMIN A.T.M. Nurul, "The Role of the Informal Sector in Economic Development: Some Evidence from Dhaka, Bangladesh", *International Labour Review*, Vol. 126, No. 5, September-October 1987.

ARTHUR YOUNG ASSOCIATES, *Informal Financial Markets: Zaire and Senegal*, draft final report prepared for US Agency for International Development, Bureau for Africa, Market Development and Investment Office under Private Enterprise Development Support Project II, Project No. 940-2028.03, Washington, D.C., March 1989.

ARYEE George, "The Informal Manufacturing Sector in Kumasi", in S.V. Sethuraman (ed.), *The Urban Informal Sector in Developing Countries: Employment, Poverty and Environment*, Geneva, ILO, 1981.

ASHE Jeffrey, *The Pisces-II Experience: Local Efforts in Micro-Enterprise Development*, Washington, D.C., US Agency for International Development, April 1985.

BENERIA Lourdes, "Sub-contracting and Employment Dynamics in Mexico City", in A. Portes, M. Castells and L.A. Benton, *The Informal Economy: Studies in Advanced and Less Developed Countries*, Baltimore, Johns Hopkins, 1989.

BERGER Marguerite, "Giving Women Credit: The Strengths and Limitations of Credit as a Tool for Alleviating Poverty", *World Development*, Vol. 17, No. 7, July 1989.

BERLINCK Manuel Tosta, *et al.*, "The Urban Informal Sector and Industrial Development in a Small City: The Case of Campinas (Brazil)", in S.V. Sethuraman (ed.), *The Urban Informal Sector in Developing Countries*, Geneva, ILO, 1981.

BHALLA A.S., "Innovations and Small Producers in Developing Countries", *Economic and Political Weekly*, February 25, 1989.

BIRKBECK Chris, "Self-Employed Proletarians in an Informal Factory: The Case of Cali's Garbage Dump", *World Development*, Vol. 6, No. 9/10, September-October 1978.

BIRKS Stace, Clive SINCLAIR and Fred FLUITMAN, *The Case of Ibadan, Nigeria*, draft report for joint ILO-World Bank-OECD Development Centre Research Project on Education and Training for Skills and Income in the Urban Informal Sector in Sub-Saharan Africa, Durham, Mountjoy Research Centre, September 1989.

BREMER-FOX Jennifer *et al.*, *An Analytical Framework for Assistance to the Informal Sector in the Sahel*, Washington, D.C., Agency for International Development, Africa Bureau, work order 43 of the ARIES Project under Contract No. DAN-1090- C-00-5124-00, November 1989.

BROMLEY Ray, "Organisation, Regulation and Exploitation in the So-Called 'Urban Informal Sector': The Street Traders of Cali, Colombia", *World Development*, Vol. 6, No. 9/10, September-October 1978.

BROMLEY Ray (ed.), *The Urban Informal Sector: Critical Perspectives on Employment and Housing Policies*, Oxford, Pergamon, 1979.

CAPECCHI Vittorio, "The Informal Economy and the Development of Flexible Specialization in Emilia-Romagna", in A. Portes, M. Castells and L.A. Benton, *The Informal Economy: Studies in Advanced and Less Developed Countries*, Baltimore, Johns Hopkins, 1989.

CAPT Josiane, *Capacité et maîtrise technologique des micro-entreprises métalliques à Bamako et Segou (Mali)*, WEP 2-29/WP 41, Geneva, ILO, October 1987.

CESM, "CESM Statistical Survey of Urban Households", Technical Paper 9 in ILO, *Growth, Employment and Equity: A Comprehensive Strategy for the Sudan*, Geneva, ILO, 1976.

CHARMES Jacques, "A Critical Review of Concepts, Definitions and Studies in the Informal Sector", in David Turnham *et al.* (eds.), *The Informal Sector Revisited*, Paris, OECD Development Centre, 1990.

DEMOL Erik and Georges NIHAN, "The Modern Informal Sector in Yaoundé", *International Labour Review*, Vol. 121, No. 1, January-February 1982.

DE SOTO Hernando, "Constraints on People: The Origins of Underground Economies and Limits to Their Growth", in Jerry Jenkins (ed.), *Beyond the Informal Sector: Including the Excluded in Developing Countries*, San Francisco, Institute for Contemporary Studies for the US Agency for International Development, 1988.

DE SOTO Hernando, *El Otro Sendero: la Revolucion Informal*, Lima, Instituto Libertad y Democracia (ILD) and Bogota, Editorial La Oveja Negra Ltda, 1986.

DE SOTO Hernando, *The Other Path: The Invisible Revolution in the Third World*, (translated by June Abbott), New York, Harper and Row, 1989.

EADES J.S., "If You Can't Beat 'em, Join 'em: State Regulation of Small Enterprises", in Ray Bromley (ed.), *Planning for Small Enterprises in Third World Cities*, Oxford, Pergamon Press, 1985.

EVERS Hans-Dieter, *Subsistence Production and Wage Labour in Jakarta*, Bielefeld (F.R. of Germany), University of Bielefeld, Faculty of Sociology, Sociology of Development Research Centre, Working Paper No. 8, 1981.

FAPOHUNDA O.J., "Human Resources and the Lagos Informal Sector", in S.V. Sethuraman (ed.), *The Urban Informal Sector in Developing Countries: Employment, Poverty and Environment*, Geneva, ILO, 1981.

FARBMAN Michael and Alan LESSIK, "The Impact of Classification on Policy", in Operations Review Unit, *Small Enterprises, New Approaches: Proceeding of the Workshop "Small Scale Enterprises Development, in Search of New Dutch Approaches"*, The Hague, Ministry of Foreign Affairs, Directorate General for International Cooperation, 1989.

FARREL Gilda, *Absorption des technologies et organisation de la production dans le secteur informel des fabrications métalliques à Quito (Equateur)*, WEP 2-22/WP 196, Geneva, ILO, January 1989.

FLAMMANG Robert A, "Informal Financial Markets in Senegal and Zaïre", paper No. 9 for Ohio State University seminar on *Informal Financial Markets in Development*, Washington, D.C., World Bank and AID, October 1989.

FLUITMAN Fred, "Training for Work in the Informal Sector: In Search of a Sensible Approach", in Fred Fluitman (ed.), *Training for Work in the Informal Sector*, Geneva, ILO, 1989.

FORTUNA Juan Carlos and Suzana PRATES, "Informal Sector Versus Informalized Labor Relations in Uruguay", in A. Portes, M. Castells and L.A. Benton, *The Informal Economy: Studies in Advanced and Less Developed Countries*, Baltimore, Johns Hopkins, 1989.

FOWLER D.A., "The Informal Sector in Freetown: Opportunities for Self-employment", in S.V. Sethuraman (ed.), *The Urban Informal Sector in Developing Countries: Employment, Poverty and Environment*, Geneva, ILO, 1981.

GERMIDIS Dimitri, Denis KESSLER and Rachel MEGHIR, "Mobilising Domestic Savings for Development: What Role for the Formal and Informal Financial Sectors", paper for Ohio State University on *Informal Financial Markets*, Paris, OECD Development Centre, CD/R (89) 8, September 1989.

GERRY Chris, *Petty Producers and the Urban Economy: A Case Study of Dakar*, World Employment Programme, Research Working Paper, WEP 2-19/WP 8, Geneva, ILO, 1974.

GOZO K.M., *Le secteur non-structuré urbain en République de Guinée : Analyse typologique, facteurs de blocage et perspectives de promotion : Rapport d'une enquête réalisée pour le compte du Gouvernement Guinéen à Conakry, Kankan, Labé et Mamou*, Addis Abeba, BIT/PECTA, 1988.

GRAHAM Douglas H., "Informal Rural Finance in Niger: Lessons for Building More Efficient and Sustainable Formal Institutions", Paper No. 4 for Ohio State University seminar on *Informal Financial Markets in Development*, Washington, D.C., World Bank and AID, October 1989.

GROWN Caren (ed.), *Beyond Survival: Expanding Income-Earning Opportunities for Women in Developing Countries*, special issue of *World Development*, Vol. 17, No. 7, July 1989.

GUERGUIL Martine, "Some Thoughts on the Definition of the Informal Sector", *CEPAL Review*, No. 35, August 1988.

GUERRERO Jaime Ramirez, "Training for Informal Sector Enterprises in Latin America", in Fred Fluitman (ed.), *Training for Work in the Informal Sector*, Geneva, ILO, 1989.

HAAN Hans, *El Sector Informal en Centroamerica: Algunas Experiencias en Proyectos, Programas y Politicas de Apoyo*, OIT, PREALC, Investigaciones sobre empleo 27, 1985.

HOUSE William J., "Labour Market Differentiation in a Developing Economy: An Example from Urban Juba, Southern Sudan", *World Development*, Vol. 15, No. 7, 1987.

HOUSE William J., "Nairobi's Informal Sector: Dynamic Entrepreneurs or Surplus Labor?", *Economic Development and Cultural Change*, Vol. 32, No. 2, January 1984.

HUGON P. *et al.*, *La petite production marchande et l'emploi dans le secteur "informel" - le cas africain*, Paris, IEDES, 1977.

ILO/ARTEP, *Urban Self-Employment in Thailand: A Study of Two Districts in Metropolitan Bangkok*, report prepared for the National Economic and Social Development Board of Thailand, New Delhi, 1988.

ILO, *Employment, Incomes and Equality: A Strategy for Increasing Productive Employment in Kenya*, Geneva, ILO, 1972.

ILO/Jobs and Skills Programme for Africa (JASPA), *Informal Sector in Africa*, Addis Abeba, 1985.

ILO, Report to Fourteenth International Conference of Labour Statisticians, October-November 1987, *Report 1: General Report*, ICLS/14/1, Geneva, ILO, 1987.

ILO, *Towards Full Employment: A programme for Colombia*, Geneva, ILO, 1970.

INTER-AMERICAN DEVELOPMENT BANK, *Seminar on Assistance to Microproducers in Latin America*, Washington, D.C., February 13-14, 1989.

JOSHI Heather, Harold LUBELL and Jean MOULY, *Abidjan: Urban Development and Employment in the Ivory Coast*, Geneva, ILO, 1973.

KILBY Peter, "Evaluating Technical Assistance", *World Development*, Vol. 7, No. 3, March 1979.

KILBY Peter and David D'ZMURA, *Searching for Benefits*, Washington, D.C., US Agency for International Development, AID Special Evaluation Study No. 28, June 1985.

KING Kenneth, "Training for the Urban Informal Sector in Developing Countries: Policy Issues for Practitioners", in Fred Fluitman (ed.), *Training for Work in the Informal Sector*, Geneva, ILO, 1989.

KUGLER Bernardo, "Estudios, Programas y Politicas del 'Sector Informal Urbano' en Colombia", *Revista de Planeacion y Desarrollo*, Vol. XIV, No. 3, Bogota, September-December 1982.

LALL Vinay D., *Informal Sector in the National Capital Region*, New Delhi, Society for Development Studies, sponsored by National Capital Region Board, Government of India, July 1987.

LEE Eddy, "The Informal Sector and Aid Policy", paper prepared for a conference on *The Informal Sector as an Integral Part of the National Economy: Research Needs and Aid Requirements*, Copenhagen, Danish Association of Development Researches and DANIDA, September 1987.

LEVITSKY Jacob, "Review of the Effectiveness of Donor Agency Support for Small Enterprise Development", in Nordic Consulting Group, *Policies for Small Enterprise Development: Papers and Proceedings of an International Conference*, Oslo, Norwegian Agency for International Development (NORAD), June 1989.

LIEDHOLM Carl and Donald MEAD, *Small Scale Industries in Developing Countries: Empirical Evidence and Policy Implications*, East Lansing, Michigan State University, Department of Agricultural Economics, MSU International Development Paper No. 9, 1987.

LIEDHOLM Carl, "Small Enterprise Dynamics and the Evolving Role of Informal Finance", Paper No. 8 for Ohio State University seminar on *Informal Financial Markets in Development*, Washington, D.C., World Bank and AID, October 1989.

LITTLE Ian, Dipak MAZUMDAR and John M. PAGE Jr, *Small Manufacturing Enterprises: A Comparative Analysis of India and Other Economies*, New York and London, Oxford University Press for the World Bank, 1987.

LUBELL Harold , "Macro-Economic Policies, Training, and the Informal Sector in Togo", December 1989, draft chapter of report by Fred Fluitman, Harold Lubell and Xavier Oudin on *Training for the Informal Sector in Togo* for joint ILO-World Bank-OECD Development Centre Research Project on Education and Training for Skills and Income in the Urban Informal Sector in Sub-Saharan Africa, (forthcoming).

LUBELL Harold and J. Douglas McCALLUM, *Bogota: Urban Development and Employment*, Geneva, ILO, 1978.

LUBELL Harold and Charbel ZAROUR , "Resilience amidst Crisis: The Informal Sector of Dakar", *International Labour Review*, Vol. 129, No. 3, June 1990.

MABOGUNJE A.L. and M.O. FILANI, "The Informal Sector in a Small City: The Case of Kano", in S.V. Sethuraman (ed.), *The Urban Informal Sector in Developing Countries: Employment, Poverty and Environment*, Geneva, ILO, 1981.

MALDONADO Carlos, "Les mal-aimés de l'économie urbaine s'organisent ; leçons d'un programme de l'OIT axé sur la participation au Mali, au Rwanda et au Togo", *Revue Internationale du Travail*, Vol. 128, No. 1, 1989. Translated as "The Underdogs of the Urban Economy Join Forces: Results of an ILO Programme in Mali, Rwanda and Togo", in *International Labour Review*, Vol. 128, No. 1, 1989.

MALDONADO Carlos, Erik DEMOL and Josiane CAPT, *Petits producteurs urbains d'Afrique francophone*, Geneva, ILO, 1987.

MAZUMDAR Dipak, "The Urban Informal Sector", *World Development*, Vol. 4, No. 8, 1976.

McKEE Katherine, "Microlevel Strategies for Supporting Livelihoods, Employment and Income Generation of Poor Women in the Third World: The Challenge of Significance", *World Development*, Vol. 17, No. 7, July 1989.

McGEE T.G., *Hawkers in Hong Kong: A Study of Planning and Policy in a Third World City*, Hong Kong, University of Hong Kong, Centre of Asian Studies, 1973.

McGEE T.G. and Y.M. YEUNG, *Hawkers in Southeast Asian Cities: Planning for the Bazaar Economy*, Ottawa, International Development Research Center (IDRC), 1977.

McKENZIE John, "Credit for the Informal Sector: An Experiment with Informal Sector Lending, and the Problems for its Institutionalisation in Senegal", paper for the Abidjan and Nairobi conferences on *The Informal Sector: Issues in Policy Reform and Programs*, organised by the Office of Technical Resources, Africa Bureau, US Agency for International Development, April 1989.

MERRICK Thomas W., "Employment and Earnings in the Informal Sector in Brazil: The Case of Belo Horizonte", *The Journal of Developing Areas*, April 1976.

NATIONAL INSTITUTE OF URBAN AFFAIRS, *Structure and Performance of Informal Enterprises: A Study of Four Cities*, New Delhi, Research Study Series No. 19, September 1987.

NIHAN Georges, Erik DEMOL and Alphonse ABODO TABI, *Le secteur non-structuré 'moderne' de Yaoundé, République-Unie du Cameroun*, Geneva, ILO, 1982.

NIHAN Georges, Erik DEMOL, David DVIRY and Comlavi JONDOH, *Le secteur non-structuré 'moderne' du Lomé, République du Togo - Rapport d'enquête et analyse des résultats*, WEP2-33 Doc. 11, Geneva, ILO, 1978.

NIHAN Georges, Erik DEMOL and Comlavi JONDOH, "The Modern Informal Sector in Lomé", in *International Labour Review*, Vol. 118, No. 5, September-October 1979.

NIHAN Georges, David DVIRY and Robert JOURDAIN, *Le secteur non-structuré 'moderne' de Nouakchott, République Islamique de Mauritanie - Support d'enquête et analyse des résultats*, WEP2-33 Doc. 4, Geneva, ILO, 1978.

NIHAN Georges, David DVIRY and Jacques SCHWARTZ, *Le secteur non-structuré de Kigali, République de Rwanda - Rapport d'enquête et analyse des résultats*, WEP 2-33, Doc. 10, Geneva, ILO, 1978.

NIHAN Georges and Robert JOURDAIN, "The Modern Informal Sector in Nouakchott", in *International Labour Review*, Vol. 117, No. 6, November-December 1978.

NIHAN Georges, Robert JOURDAIN and H. SIDIBE, *Le secteur non-structuré 'moderne' de Bamako, République du Mali - Synthèse des résultats de l'enquête*, WEP2-33, Doc. 14, Geneva, ILO, 1979.

OECD DEVELOPMENT CENTRE, *Programme of Research 1990-1992*, Paris, November 1989.

OFISEL Ltda, *El Sector Informal en la Economia Urbana de Bogotá*, WEP2-19/WP25, Geneva, ILO, August 1977.

OHIO STATE UNIVERSITY, *Informal Financial Markets in Development*, papers for seminar sponsored by the World Bank and AID and held in Washington, D.C., October, 18-20, 1989.

PORTES A., S. BLITZER and J. CURTIS, "The Urban Informal Sector in Uruguay: Its Internal Structure, Characteristics, and Effects", *World Development*, Vol. 14, No. 6, June 1986.

PORTES A., M. CASTELLS and L.A. BENTON, *The Informal Economy: Studies in Advanced and Less Developed Countries*, Baltimore, Johns Hopkins, 1989.

POSNER Jill, *Street Foods in Senegal*, Washington, D.C., Equity Policy Center, 1983.

PREALC, *Sector Informal: Funcionamiento y Politicas*, Santiago, ILO/PREALC, 1978.

PREALC, *Sobrevivir en la Calle: El Comercio Ambulante en Santiago*, Santiago, ILO/PREALC, 1988.

ROBERTS Bryan R., "Employment Structure, Life Cycle, and Life Chances: Formal and Informal Sectors in Guadalajara", in A. Portes, M. Castells and L.A. Benton, *The Informal Economy: Studies in Advanced and Less Developed Countries*, Baltimore, Johns Hopkins, 1989.

REPUBLICA ARGENTINA, Ministerio de Trabajo y Seguridad Social, Direccion Nacional de Recursos Humanos y Empleo, *El Sector Cuenta Propria: Estudio Socioeconomico del Trabajo Independiente y de la Miniempresa en la Capital Federal y en el Gran Buenos Aires (1980)*, Buenos Aires, PNUD/OIT, ARG/87/003, 1981.

SANCHEZ Carlos *et al.*, "The Informal and Quasi-informal Sectors in Córdoba (Argentina)", in S.V. Sethuraman (ed.), *The Urban Informal Sector in Developing Countries*, Geneva, ILO, 1981.

SANDERATNE Nimal, "Informal Lenders in Sri Lanka: Linking Formal and Informal Sectors", Paper No. 10 for Ohio State University seminar on *Informal Financial Markets in Development*, Washington, D.C., World Bank and AID, October 1989.

SASSEN-KOOB Saskia , "New York City's Informal Economy", in A. Portes, M. Castells and L.A. Benton, *The Informal Economy: Studies in Advanced and Less Developed Countries*, Baltimore, Johns Hopkins, 1989.

SCHRIEDER Gertrud and Carlos E. CUEVAS, "Taking Over the Monetized Economy: Informal Financial Groups in Cameroon", paper No. 20 for Ohio State University seminar on *Informal Financial Markets*, Washington, D.C., World Bank and AID, October 1989.

SETHURAMAN S.V., "Concepts, Methodology and Scope", Chapter 2 of S.V. Sethuraman (ed.), *The Urban Informal Sector in Developing Countries: Employment, Poverty and Environment*, Geneva, ILO, 1981a.

SETHURAMAN S.V., "Summary and Conclusions: Implications for Policy and Action", Chapter 14 of S.V. Sethuraman (ed.), *The Urban Informal Sector in Developing Countries: Employment, Poverty and Environment*, Geneva, ILO, 1981b.

SETHURAMAN S.V., *Survey Instrument for a Study of the Urban Informal Sector: The Case of Jakarta*, Geneva, ILO, 1974.

SETHURAMAN S.V. (ed.), *The Urban Informal Sector in Developing Countries: Employment, Poverty and Environment*, Geneva, ILO, 1981c.

SHIPTON Parker, "The Rope and the Box: Gambian Saving Strategies and What They Imply for International Aid in the Sahel", Paper No. 18 for Ohio State University seminar on *Informal Financial Markets in Development*, Washington, D.C., World Bank and AID, October 1989.

SOUZA Paulo R. and Victor E. TOKMAN, "The Informal Urban Sector in Latin America", *International Labour Review*, Vol. 114, No. 3, November-December 1976.

STEPICK Alex, "Miami's Two Informal Sectors", in A. Portes, M. Castells and L.A. Benton, *The Informal Economy: Studies in Advanced and Less Developed Countries*, Baltimore, Johns Hopkins, 1989.

TESZLER Roger and Klaas MOLENAAR, "In Search of New Approaches: Major Areas of Attention", in Operations Review Unit, *Small Enterprises, New Approaches: Proceedings of the Workshop "Small Scale Enterprise Development, in Search of New Dutch Approaches"*, The Hague, Ministry of Foreign Affairs, Directorate General for International Cooperation, 1989.

TINKER Irene *et al.*, *Utilizing the Street Food Trade in Development Programming: Final Report*, Washington, D.C., Equity Policy Center (EPOC) for US Agency for International Development under Grant NOTR-0200-GSS-1225-03, March 1985.

TOKMAN Victor E., "Competition between the Informal and Formal Sectors in Retailing: The Case of Santiago", in *The Urban Informal Sector: Critical Perspectives*, special issue of *World Development*, Vol. 6, No. 9, September-October 1978a.

TOKMAN Victor E., "Policies for a Heterogeneous Informal Sector in Latin America", *World Development*, Vol. 17, No. 7, July 1989.

TOKMAN Victor E., "Politicas para el Sector Informal Urbano en América Latina", *Revista Internacional de Trabajo*, Vol. 97, No. 3, July-September 1978b.

TOKMAN Victor E., "The Informal Sector in Latin America: 15 Years Later", in David Turnham *et al.*, (eds.), *The Informal Sector Revisited*, Paris, OECD Development Centre, 1990.

TOURE Abdou, *Les petits métiers à Abidjan*, Paris, Karthala, 1987.

TURNHAM David, Bernard SALOME and Antoine SCHWARZ (ed.), *The Informal Sector Revisited*, Paris, OECD Development Centre, 1990.

UNDP/GOVERNMENT OF NETHERLANDS/ILO/UNIDO, *Development of Small Rural Enterprise: Lessons from Experience*, Vienne, UNIDO, 1988.

US AGENCY FOR INTERNATIONAL DEVELOPMENT, *AID Micro-Enterprise Stock Taking: Synthesis Report* (draft), Washington, D.C., AID, Bureau for Program and Policy Coordination, Center for Development Information and Evaluation, AID Evaluation Occasional Paper, March 1989.

VAN DIJK M.P., *Burkina Faso : Le secteur informel de Ouagadougou*, Paris, L'Harmattan, 1986.

VARDON Jean, Jean-Pierre JAROUSSE and Alain MINGAT, *Formation et revenus dans le secteur informel : l'exemple de l'artisanat et du petit commerce urbain à Nyamey*, draft report for joint ILO-World Bank-OECD Development Centre Research Project on Education and Training for Skills and Income in the Urban Informal Sector in Sub-Saharan Africa, 1989.

WILLARD Jean-Charles, "L'économie souterraine dans les comptes nationaux", in *Economie et Statistique*, No. 226, November 1989.

WORLD BANK, Africa Region, Technical Department, *Africa Regional Programme on Enterprise Development: Research and Development Programme Proposal*, Washington, D.C., February 1990.

WORLD BANK, *Senegal Public Works and Employment Project: Staff Appraisal Report*, Washington, D.C., November, 3, 1989.

YBARRA Josep-Antoni, "Informalization in the Valencian Economy: A Model for Underdevelopment", in A. Portes, M. Castells and L.A. Benton, *The Informal Economy: Studies in Advanced and Less Developed Countries*, Baltimore, Johns Hopkins, 1989.

ZAROUR Charbel, *Etude du secteur informel de Dakar et de ses environs : Rapport final*, Dakar, USAID/SENEGAL, August 1989.

ZAROUR Charbel, *Systèmes de crédit et de mobilisation de l'épargne en milieu rural : Le rôle des O.N.G. et autres structures d'intervention*, Dakar, USAID, March 1988.

WHERE TO OBTAIN OECD PUBLICATIONS – OÙ OBTENIR LES PUBLICATIONS DE L'OCDE

Argentina – Argentine
Carlos Hirsch S.R.L.
Galería Güemes, Florida 165, 4° Piso
1333 Buenos Aires   Tel. 30.7122, 331.1787 y 331.2391
Telegram: Hirsch–Baires
Telex: 21112 UAPE–AR. Ref. s/2901
Telefax:(1)331–1787

Australia – Australie
D.A. Book (Aust.) Pty. Ltd.
648 Whitehorse Road, P.O.B 163
Mitcham, Victoria 3132   Tel. (03)873.4411
Telex: AA37911 DA BOOK
Telefax: (03)873.5679

Austria – Autriche
OECD Publications and Information Centre
Schedestrasse 7
5300 Bonn 1 (Germany)   Tel. (0228)21.60.45
Telefax: (0228)26.11.04

Gerold & Co.
Graben 31
Wien I   Tel. (0222)533.50.14

Belgium – Belgique
Jean De Lannoy
Avenue du Roi 202
B–1060 Bruxelles   Tel. (02)538.51.69/538.08.41
Telex: 63220   Telefax: (02) 538.08.41

Canada
Renouf Publishing Company Ltd.
1294 Algoma Road
Ottawa, ON K1B 3W8   Tel. (613)741.4333
Telex: 053–4783   Telefax: (613)741.5439
Stores:
61 Sparks Street
Ottawa, ON K1P 5R1   Tel. (613)238.8985
211 Yonge Street
Toronto, ON M5B 1M4   Tel. (416)363.3171

Federal Publications
165 University Avenue
Toronto, ON M5H 3B8   Tel. (416)581.1552
Telefax: (416)581.1743

Les Publications Fédérales
1185 rue de l'Université
Montréal, PQ H3B 3A7   Tel.(514)954–1633

Les Éditions La Liberté Inc.
3020 Chemin Sainte–Foy
Sainte–Foy, PQ G1X 3V6   Tel. (418)658.3763
Telefax: (418)658.3763

Denmark – Danemark
Munksgaard Export and Subscription Service
35, Norre Sogade, P.O. Box 2148
DK–1016 Kobenhavn K   Tel. (45 33)12.85.70
Telex: 19431 MUNKS DK   Telefax: (45 33)12.93.87

Finland – Finlande
Akateeminen Kirjakauppa
Keskuskatu 1, P.O. Box 128
00100 Helsinki   Tel. (358 0)12141
Telex: 125080   Telefax: (358 0)121.4441

France
OECD/OCDE
Mail Orders/Commandes par correspondance:
2 rue André–Pascal
75775 Paris Cedex 16   Tel. (1)45.24.82.00
Bookshop/Librairie:
33, rue Octave–Feuillet
75016 Paris   Tel. (1)45.24.81.67
    (1)45.24.81.81
Telex: 620 160 OCDE
Telefax: (33–1)45.24.85.00

Librairie de l'Université
12a, rue Nazareth
13090 Aix–en–Provence   Tel. 42.26.18.08

Germany – Allemagne
OECD Publications and Information Centre
Schedestrasse 7
5300 Bonn 1   Tel. (0228)21.60.45
Telefax: (0228)26.11.04

Greece – Grèce
Librairie Kauffmann
28 rue du Stade
105 64 Athens   Tel. 322.21.60
Telex: 218187 LIKA Gr

Hong Kong
Swindon Book Co. Ltd.
13 – 15 Lock Road
Kowloon, Hongkong   Tel. 366 80 31
Telex: 50 441 SWIN HX
Telefax: 739 49 75

Iceland – Islande
Mál Mog Menning
Laugavegi 18, Pósthólf 392
121 Reykjavik   Tel. 15199/24240

India – Inde
Oxford Book and Stationery Co.
Scindia House
New Delhi 110001   Tel. 331.5896/5308
Telex: 31 61990 AM IN
Telefax: (11)332.5993
17 Park Street
Calcutta 700016   Tel. 240832

Indonesia – Indonésie
Pdii–Lipi
P.O. Box 269/JKSMG/88
Jakarta 12790   Tel. 583467
Telex: 62 875

Ireland – Irlande
TDC Publishers – Library Suppliers
12 North Frederick Street
Dublin 1   Tel. 744835/749677
Telex: 33530 TDCP EI   Telefax : 748416

Italy – Italie
Libreria Commissionaria Sansoni
Via Benedetto Fortini, 120/10
Casella Post. 552
50125 Firenze   Tel. (055)645415
Telex: 570466   Telefax: (39.55)641257
Via Bartolini 29
20155 Milano   Tel. 365083
La diffusione delle pubblicazioni OCSE viene assicurata dalle
principali librerie ed anche da:
Editrice e Libreria Herder
Piazza Montecitorio 120
00186 Roma   Tel. 679.4628
Telex: NATEL I 621427
Libreria Hoepli
Via Hoepli 5
20121 Milano   Tel. 865446
Telex: 31.33.95 Telefax: (39.2)805.2886
Libreria Scientifica
Dott. Lucio de Biasio "Aeiou"
Via Meravigli 16
20123 Milano   Tel. 807679
Telex: 800175

Japan – Japon
OECD Publications and Information Centre
Landic Akasaka Building
2–3–4 Akasaka, Minato–ku
Tokyo 107   Tel. (81.3)3586.2016
Telefax: (81.3)3584.7929

Korea – Corée
Kyobo Book Centre Co. Ltd.
P.O. Box 1658, Kwang Hwa Moon
Seoul   Tel. (REP)730.78.91
Telefax: 735.0030

Malaysia/Singapore – Malaisie/Singapour
Co–operative Bookshop Ltd.
University of Malaya
P.O. Box 1127, Jalan Pantai Baru
59700 Kuala Lumpur
Malaysia   Tel. 756.5000/756.5425
Telefax: 757.3661

Information Publications Pte. Ltd.
Pei–Fu Industrial Building
24 New Industrial Road No. 02–06
Singapore 1953   Tel. 283.1786/283.1798
Telefax: 284.8875

Netherlands – Pays–Bas
SDU Uitgeverij
Christoffel Plantijnstraat 2
Postbus 20014
2500 EA's–Gravenhage   Tel. (070 3)78.99.11
Voor bestellingen: Tel. (070 3)78.98.80
Telex: 32486 stdru   Telefax: (070 3)47.63.51

New Zealand – Nouvelle–Zélande
Government Printing Office
Customer Services
33 The Esplanade – P.O. Box 38–900
Petone, Wellington
Tel. (04) 685–555   Telefax: (04)685–333

Norway – Norvège
Narvesen Info Center – NIC
Bertrand Narvesens vei 2
P.O. Box 6125 Etterstad
0602 Oslo 6   Tel. (02)57.33.00
Telex: 79668 NIC N   Telefax: (02)68.19.01

Pakistan
Mirza Book Agency
65 Shahrah Quaid–E–Azam
Lahore 3   Tel. 66839
Telex: 44886 UBL PK. Attn: MIRZA BK

Portugal
Livraria Portugal
Rua do Carmo 70–74
Apart. 2681
1117 Lisboa Codex   Tel. 347.49.82/3/4/5
Telefax: 37 02 64

Singapore/Malaysia – Singapour/Malaisie
See "Malaysia/Singapore" – "Voir "Malaisie/Singapour"

Spain – Espagne
Mundi–Prensa Libros S.A.
Castelló 37, Apartado 1223
Madrid 28001   Tel. (91) 431.33.99
Telex: 49370 MPLI   Telefax: 575 39 98
Libreria Internacional AEDOS
Consejo de Ciento 391
08009 –Barcelona   Tel. (93) 301–86–15
Telefax: (93) 317–01–41

Sweden – Suède
Fritzes Fackboksföretaget
Box 16356, S 103 27 STH
Regeringsgatan 12
DS Stockholm   Tel. (08)23.89.00
Telex: 12387 Telefax: (08)20.50.21

Subscription Agency/Abonnements:
Wennergren–Williams AB
Nordenflychtsvagen 74
Box 30004
104 25 Stockholm   Tel. (08)13.67.00
Telex: 19937 Telefax: (08)618.62.36

Switzerland – Suisse
OECD Publications and Information Centre
Schedestrasse 7
5300 Bonn 1 (Germany)   Tel. (0228)21.60.45
Telefax: (0228)26.11.04

Librairie Payot
6 rue Grenus
1211 Genève 11   Tel. (022)731.89.50
Telex: 28356
Subscription Agency – Service des Abonnements
4 place Pépinet – BP 3312
1002 Lausanne   Tel. (021)341.33.31
Telefax: (021)341.33.45

Maditec S.A.
Ch. des Palettes 4
1020 Renens/Lausanne   Tel. (021)635.08.65
Telefax: (021)635.07.80
United Nations Bookshop/Librairie des Nations–Unies
Palais des Nations
1211 Genève 10   Tel. (022)734.60.11 (ext. 48.72)
Telex: 289696 (Attn: Sales)
Telefax: (022)733.98.79

Taiwan – Formose
Good Faith Worldwide Int'l. Co. Ltd.
9th Floor, No. 118, Sec. 2
Chung Hsiao E. Road
Taipei   Tel. 391.7396/391.7397
Telefax: (02) 394.9176

Thailand – Thaïlande
Suksit Siam Co. Ltd.
1715 Rama IV Road, Samyan
Bangkok 5   Tel. 251.1630

Turkey – Turquie
Kültur Yayinlari Is–Türk Ltd. Sti.
Atatürk Bulvari No. 191/Kat. 21
Kavaklidere/Ankara   Tel. 25.07.60
Dolmabahce Cad. No. 29
Besiktas/Istanbul   Tel. 160.71.88
Telex: 43482B

United Kingdom – Royaume–Uni
HMSO
Gen. enquiries   Tel. (071) 873 0011
Postal orders only:
P.O. Box 276, London SW8 5DT
Personal Callers HMSO Bookshop
49 High Holborn, London WC1V 6HB
Telex: 297138 Telefax: 071 873 8463
Branches at: Belfast, Birmingham, Bristol, Edinburgh,
Manchester

United States – États–Unis
OECD Publications and Information Centre
2001 L Street N.W., Suite 700
Washington, D.C. 20036–4095   Tel. (202)785.6323
Telefax: (202)785.0350

Venezuela
Libreria del Este
Avda F. Miranda 52, Aptdo. 60337
Edificio Galipán
Caracas 106   Tel. 951.1705/951.2307/951.1297
Telegram: Libreste Caracas

Yugoslavia – Yougoslavie
Jugoslovenska Knjiga
Knez Mihajlova 2, P.O. Box 36
Beograd   Tel. (011)621.992
Telex: 12466 jk bgd   Telefax: (011)625.970

Orders and inquiries from countries where Distributors have
not yet been appointed should be sent to: OECD Publications
Service, 2 rue André–Pascal, 75775 Paris Cedex 16, France.
Les commandes provenant de pays où l'OCDE n'a pas encore
désigné de distributeur devraient être adressées à : OCDE,
Service des Publications, 2, rue André–Pascal, 75775 Paris
Cedex 16, France.

12/90

OECD PUBLICATIONS, 2 rue André–Pascal, 75775 PARIS CEDEX 16
PRINTED IN FRANCE
(41 91 08 1) ISBN 92–64–13475–1 – No. 45505 1991